Microsoft® PowerPoint® 4.0 for Windows™ Illustrated Brief Edition

David W. Beskeen
Steven M. Johnson

Course Technology, Inc. *One Main Street, Cambridge, MA 02142*

An International Thomson Publishing Company

Albany • Bonn • Boston • Cincinnati • London • Madrid • Melbourne • Mexico City
New York • Paris • San Francisco • Singapore • Tokyo • Toronto • Washington

Microsoft PowerPoint 4.0 for Windows — Illustrated Brief Edition is published by Course Technology, Inc.

Managing Editor: Marjorie Schlaikjer
Product Manager: Nicole Jones Pinard
Production Supervisor: Kathryn Dinovo
Text Designer: Leslie Hartwell
Cover Designer: John Gamache

For more information contact:
Course Technology, Inc.
One Main Street
Cambridge, MA 02142

International Thomson Publishing Europe
Berkshire House 168-173
High Holborn
London WCIV 7AA
England

Thomas Nelson Australia
102 Dodds Street
South Melbourne, 3205
Victoria, Australia

Nelson Canada
1120 Birchmount Road
Scarborough, Ontario
Canada M1K 5G4

International Thomson Editores
Campos Eliseos 385, Piso 7
Col. Polanco
11560 Mexico D.F. Mexico

International Thomson Publishing GmbH
Königswinterer Strasse 418
53227 Bonn
Germany

International Thomson Publishing Asia
211 Henderson Road
#05-10 Henderson Building
Singapore 0315

International Thomson Publishing Japan
Hirakawacho Kyowa Building, 3F
2-2-1 Hirakawacho
Chiyoda-ku, Tokyo 102
Japan

Trademarks

Disclaimer

ISBN 1-56527-593-4

Printed in the United States of America

10 9 8 7 6 5 4 3 2 1

From the Publisher

At Course Technology, Inc., we believe that technology will transform the way that people teach and learn. We are very excited about bringing you, instructors and students, the most practical and affordable technology-related products available.

The Course Technology Development Process

Our development process is unparalleled in the educational publishing industry. Every product we create goes through an exacting process of design, development, review, and testing.

Reviewers give us direction and insight that shape our manuscripts and bring them up to the latest standards. Every manuscript is quality tested. Students whose background matches the intended audience work through every keystroke, carefully checking for clarity and pointing out errors in logic and sequence. Together with our technical reviewers, these testers help us ensure that everything that carries our name is as error-free and easy to use as possible.

Course Technology Products

We show both *how* and *why* technology is critical to solving problems in the classroom and in whatever field you choose to teach or pursue. Our time-tested, step-by-step instructions provide unparalleled clarity. Examples and applications are chosen and crafted to motivate students.

The Course Technology Team

This book will suit your needs because it was delivered quickly, efficiently, and affordably. In every aspect of business, we rely on a commitment to quality and the use of technology. Every employee contributes to this process. The names of all our employees are listed below: Tim Ashe, David Backer, Stephen M. Bayle, Josh Bernoff, Michelle Brown, Ann Marie Buconjic, Jody Buttafoco, Kerry Cannell, Jim Chrysikos, Barbara Clemens, Susan Collins, John M. Connolly, Kim Crowley, Myrna D'Addario, Lisa D'Alessandro, Jodi Davis, Howard S. Diamond, Kathryn Dinovo, Joseph B. Dougherty, MaryJane Dwyer, Chris Elkhill, Don Fabricant, Jeff Goding, Laurie Gomes, Eileen Gorham, Andrea Greitzer, Catherine Griffin, Tim Hale, Jamie Harper, Roslyn Hooley, John Hope, Matt Kenslea, Susannah Lean, Laurie Lindgren, Kim Mai, Margaret Makowski, Elizabeth Martinez, Debbie Masi, Don Maynard, Dan Mayo, Kathleen McCann, Jay McNamara, Mac Mendelsohn, Kim Munsell, Amy Oliver, Michael Ormsby, Kristine Otto, Debbie Parlee, Kristin Patrick, Charlie Patsios, Darren Perl, Kevin Phaneuf, George J. Pilla, Nicole Jones Pinard, Cathy Prindle, Nancy Ray, Marjorie Schlaikjer, Christine Spillett, Michelle Tucker, David Upton, Mark Valentine, Karen Wadsworth, Anne Marie Walker, Renee Walkup, Tracy Wells, Donna Whiting, Janet Wilson, Lisa Yameen.

Preface

Course Technology, Inc. is proud to present this new book in its Illustrated Series. *Microsoft PowerPoint 4.0 for Windows — Illustrated Brief Edition* provides a highly visual, hands-on introduction to Microsoft PowerPoint. The book is designed as a learning tool for PowerPoint novices but will also be useful as a source for future reference. It assumes students have learned basic Windows skills and file management from *Microsoft Windows 3.1 Illustrated* or from an equivalent book.

Organization and Coverage

Microsoft PowerPoint 4.0 for Windows — Illustrated Brief Edition contains four units that cover basic PowerPoint skills. In these units students learn how to plan, define, create, and modify presentations. They work with text and objects, and learn how to create an on-screen slide show.

Approach

Microsoft PowerPoint 4.0 for Windows — Illustrated Brief Edition distinguishes itself from other textbooks with its highly visual approach to computer instruction.

Lessons: Information Displays

The basic lesson format of this text is the "information display," a two-page lesson that is sharply focused on a specific task. This sharp focus and the precise beginning and end of a lesson make it easy for students to study specific material. Modular lessons are less overwhelming for students, and they provide instructors with more flexibility in planning classes and assigning specific work. The units are modular as well and can be presented in any order.

Each lesson, or "information display," contains the following elements:

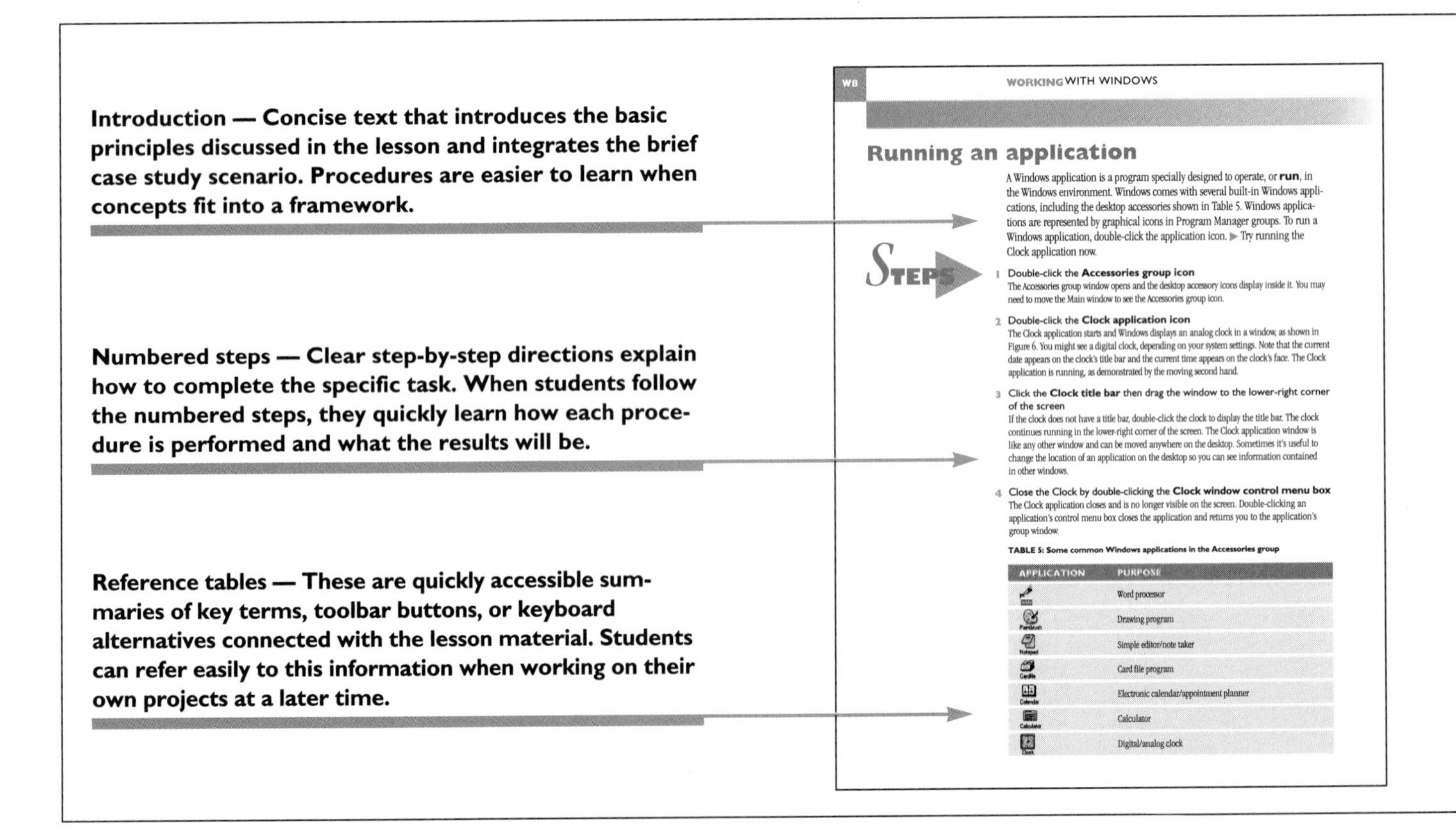
Introduction — Concise text that introduces the basic principles discussed in the lesson and integrates the brief case study scenario. Procedures are easier to learn when concepts fit into a framework.
Numbered steps — Clear step-by-step directions explain how to complete the specific task. When students follow the numbered steps, they quickly learn how each procedure is performed and what the results will be.
Reference tables — These are quickly accessible summaries of key terms, toolbar buttons, or keyboard alternatives connected with the lesson material. Students can refer easily to this information when working on their own projects at a later time.
STEPS

W8 WORKING WITH WINDOWS

Running an application

A Windows application is a program specially designed to operate, or **run**, in the Windows environment. Windows comes with several built-in Windows applications, including the desktop accessories shown in Table 5. Windows applications are represented by graphical icons in Program Manager groups. To run a Windows application, double-click the application icon. ▶ Try running the Clock application now.

1. Double-click the **Accessories group icon**
   The Accessories group window opens and the desktop accessory icons display inside it. You may need to move the Main window to see the Accessories group icon.
2. Double-click the **Clock application icon**
   The Clock application starts and Windows displays an analog clock in a window, as shown in Figure 6. You might see a digital clock, depending on your system settings. Note that the current date appears on the clock's title bar and the current time appears on the clock's face. The Clock application is running, as demonstrated by the moving second hand.
3. Click the **Clock title bar** then drag the window to the lower-right corner of the screen
   If the clock does not have a title bar, double-click the clock to display the title bar. The clock continues running in the lower-right corner of the screen. The Clock application window is like any other window and can be moved anywhere on the desktop. Sometimes it's useful to change the location of an application on the desktop so you can see information contained in other windows.
4. Close the Clock by double-clicking the **Clock window control menu box**
   The Clock application closes and is no longer visible on the screen. Double-clicking an application's control menu box closes the application and returns you to the application's group window.

TABLE 5: Some common Windows applications in the Accessories group

APPLICATION	PURPOSE
	Word processor
Paintbrush	Drawing program
Notepad	Simple editor/note taker
Cardfile	Card file program
Calendar	Electronic calendar/appointment planner
Calculator	Calculator
Clock	Digital/analog clock

Features

Microsoft PowerPoint 4.0 for Windows — Illustrated Brief Edition is an exceptional textbook because it contains the following features:

- "Read This Before You Begin PowerPoint 4.0" Page — This page provides essential information that both students and instructors need to know before they begin working through the units.
- Real-World Case — The case study used throughout the textbook is designed to be "real-world" in nature and representative of the kinds of activities that students will encounter when working with presentation graphics software. With a real-world case, the process of solving the problem will be more meaningful to students.
- End of Unit Material — Each unit concludes with a meaningful Concepts Review that tests students' understanding of what they learned in the unit. The Concepts Review is followed by an Applications Review, which provides students with additional hands-on practice of the skills they learned in the unit. The Applications Review is followed by Independent Challenges, which pose case problems for students to solve. The Independent Challenges allow students to learn by exploring, and develop critical thinking skills.

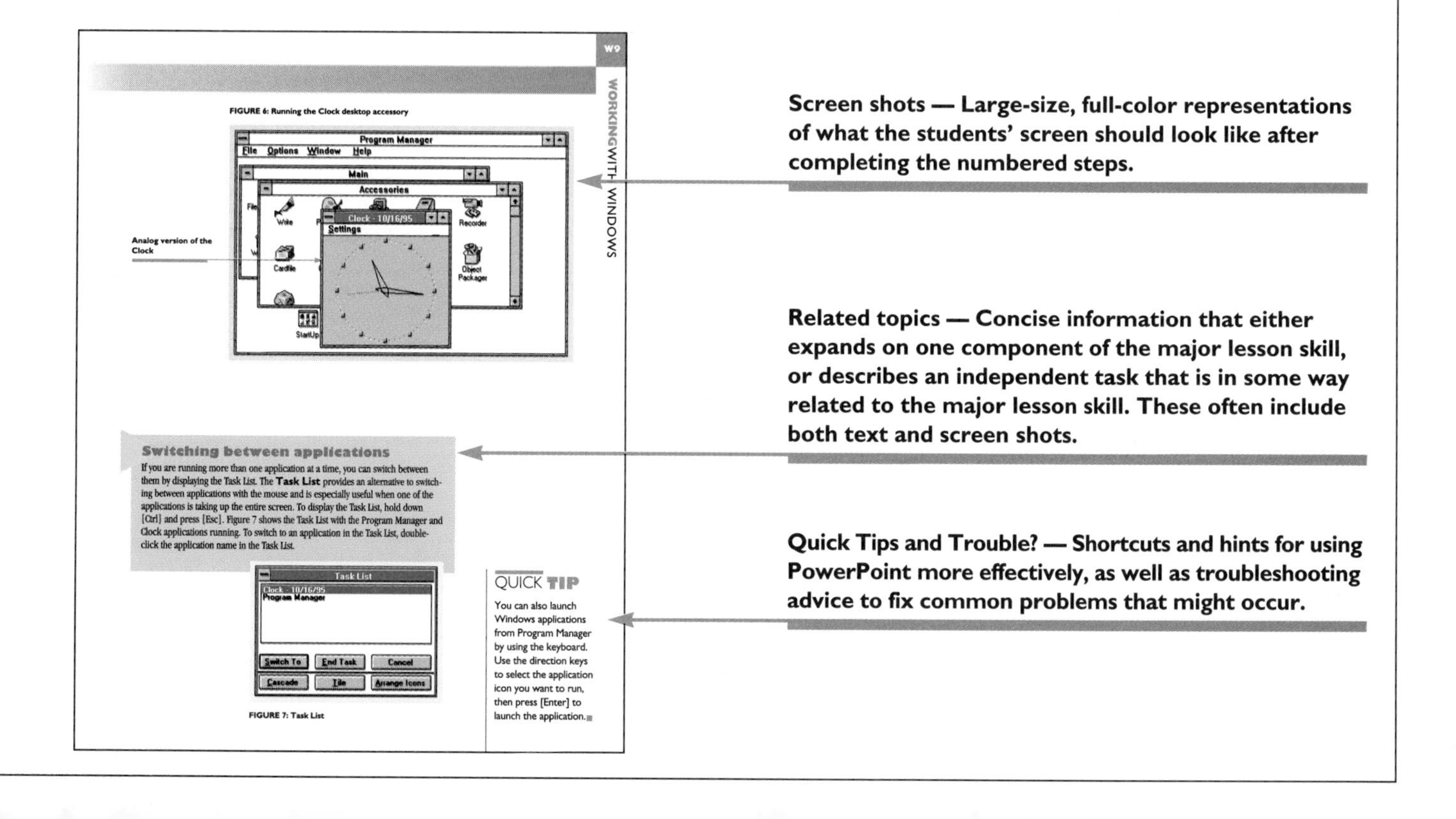
W9
WORKING WITH WINDOWS
FIGURE 6: Running the Clock desktop accessory
Analog version of the Clock
Switching between applications
FIGURE 7: Task List
QUICK TIP
You can also launch Windows applications from Program Manager by using the keyboard. Use the direction keys to select the application icon you want to run, then press [Enter] to launch the application.
Screen shots — Large-size, full-color representations of what the students' screen should look like after completing the numbered steps.
Related topics — Concise information that either expands on one component of the major lesson skill, or describes an independent task that is in some way related to the major lesson skill. These often include both text and screen shots.
Quick Tips and Trouble? — Shortcuts and hints for using PowerPoint more effectively, as well as troubleshooting advice to fix common problems that might occur.

The Student Disk

The Student Disk bundled with the instructor's copy of this book contains all the data files students need to complete the step-by-step lessons.

Adopters of this text are granted the right to post the Student Disk on any standalone computer or network used by students who have purchased this product.

For more information on the Student Disk, see the page in this book called "Read This Before You Begin Microsoft PowerPoint 4.0."

The Supplements

Instructor's Manual — The Instructor's Manual is quality assurance tested. It includes:

- Solutions to all lessons, Concept Reviews, Application Reviews, and Independent Challenges
- A disk containing solutions to all of the lessons, Concept Reviews, Application Reviews, and Independent Challenges
- Unit notes, which contain tips from the author about the instructional progression of each lesson
- Extra problems
- Transparency masters of key concepts

Test Bank — The Test Bank contains approximately 50 questions per unit in true/false, multiple choice, and fill-in-the-blank formats, plus two essay questions. Each question has been quality assurance tested by students to achieve clarity and accuracy.

Electronic Test Bank — The Electronic Test Bank allows instructors to edit individual test questions, select questions individually or at random, and print out scrambled versions of the same test to any supported printer.

Acknowledgments

Steve and I would like to thank the entire Course Technology team for their support and direction on this project. Special thanks to Nicole Jones Pinard for her diligence in coordinating and managing this complex project.

We would also like to especially thank Joan Carey, our developmental editor, for her insight and editorial expertise, which helped produce this quality instructional book.

David W. Beskeen
Steven M. Johnson

Contents

TABLES

Microsoft® PowerPoint® 4.0

for Windows™

Read This Before You Begin Microsoft PowerPoint 4.0

To the Student

The lessons and exercises in this book feature several PowerPoint presentation files provided to your instructor. To complete the step-by-step lessons, Applications Reviews, and Independent Challenges in this book, you must have a Student Disk. Your instructor will do one of the following: 1) provide you with your own copy of the disk; 2) have you copy it from the network onto your own floppy disk; or 3) have you copy the lesson files from a network into your own subdirectory on the network. Always use your own copies of the lesson and exercise files. See your instructor or technical support person for further information.

Using Your Own Computer

If you are going to work through this book using your own computer, you need a computer system running Microsoft Windows 3.1, Microsoft PowerPoint 4.0 for Windows, and a Student Disk. *You will not be able to complete the step-by-step lessons in this book using your own computer until you have your own Student Disk.* This book assumes the default settings under a complete installation of Microsoft PowerPoint 4.0 for Windows.

To the Instructor

Bundled with the instructor's copy of this book is a Student Disk. The Student Disk contains all the files your students need to complete the step-by-step lessons in the units, Applications Reviews, and Independent Challenges. As an adopter of this text, you are granted the right to distribute the files on the Student Disk to any student who has purchased a copy of the text. You are free to post all these files to a network or standalone workstations, or simply provide copies of the disk to your students. The instructions in this book assume that the students know which drive and directory contain the Student Disk, so it's important that you provide disk location information before the students start working through the units. This book also assumes that PowerPoint 4.0 is set up using the complete installation procedure.

Using the Student Disk files

To keep the original files on the Student Disk intact, the instructions in this book for opening files require two important steps: (1) Open the existing file and (2) Save it as a new file with a new name. This procedure, covered in the lesson entitled "Opening an existing presentation," ensures that the original file will remain unmodified in case the student wants to redo any lesson or exercise.

To organize their files, students are instructed to save their files to the MY_FILES directory on their Student Disk that they created in *Microsoft Windows 3.1 Illustrated*. In case your students did not complete this lesson, it is included in the Instructor's Manual that accompanies this book. You can circulate this to your students or you can instruct them to simply save to drive A or drive B.

UNIT 1

OBJECTIVES

- Define presentation software
- Start PowerPoint 4.0 for Windows
- Use the AutoContent Wizard
- View the PowerPoint window
- View your presentation
- Work with toolbars
- Get Help
- Close a file and exit PowerPoint

Getting Started WITH MICROSOFT POWERPOINT 4.0

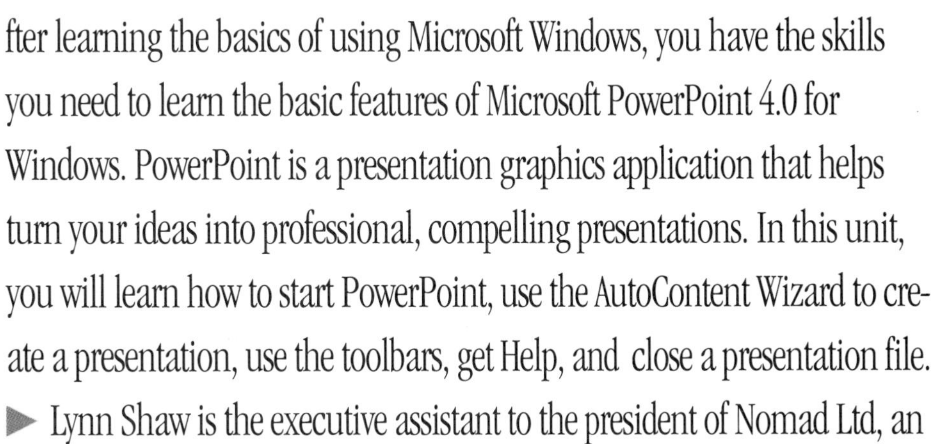

After learning the basics of using Microsoft Windows, you have the skills you need to learn the basic features of Microsoft PowerPoint 4.0 for Windows. PowerPoint is a presentation graphics application that helps turn your ideas into professional, compelling presentations. In this unit, you will learn how to start PowerPoint, use the AutoContent Wizard to create a presentation, use the toolbars, get Help, and close a presentation file. ▶ Lynn Shaw is the executive assistant to the president of Nomad Ltd, an outdoor sporting gear and adventure travel company. To create more effective presentations, she wants to familiarize herself with the basics of PowerPoint and learn how to use PowerPoint. ▶

Defining presentation software

A **presentation graphics application** is a computer program you use to organize and present information. Whether you are giving a sales pitch or promoting a product, a presentation graphics application can help make your presentation effective and professional. You can use PowerPoint to create 35-mm slides, overheads, speaker's notes, audience handouts, outline pages, or on-screen presentations, depending on your specific presentation needs. Table 1-1 explains the PowerPoint output capabilities. ▶ Nomad's president has asked Lynn Shaw to create a brief presentation on the company's annual report. Lynn is not that familiar with PowerPoint so she gets right to work exploring PowerPoint. Figure 1-1 shows an overhead Lynn created using a word processor for the president's most recent presentation. Figure 1-2 shows how the same overhead might look in PowerPoint.

These are some of the benefits Lynn will gain by using PowerPoint:

- **Enter and edit data easily**
  Using PowerPoint, Lynn can enter and edit data quickly and efficiently. When Lynn needs to change a part of her presentation, she can use PowerPoint's advanced word processing and outlining capabilities to edit her content rather than re-create her presentation.

- **Change the appearance of information**
  By exploring PowerPoint's capabilities, Lynn will discover how easy it is to change the appearance of her presentation. PowerPoint has many features that can transform the way text, graphics, and slides appear.

- **Organize and arrange information**
  Once Lynn starts using PowerPoint, she won't have to spend a lot of time making sure her information is correct and in the right order. With PowerPoint, Lynn can quickly and easily rearrange and modify any piece of information in her presentation.

- **Incorporate information from other sources**
  When Lynn creates presentations, she often uses information from other people in the company. Using PowerPoint, she can import information from a variety of sources, including spreadsheets, graphics, and word processed files from applications such as Microsoft Word, Microsoft Excel, Microsoft Access, and WordPerfect.

- **Show a presentation on any Windows computer**
  PowerPoint has a powerful feature called the **PowerPoint Viewer** that Lynn can use to show her presentation on computers that do not have PowerPoint installed. The PowerPoint Viewer displays a presentation as an on-screen slide show.

FIGURE 1-1: Traditional overhead

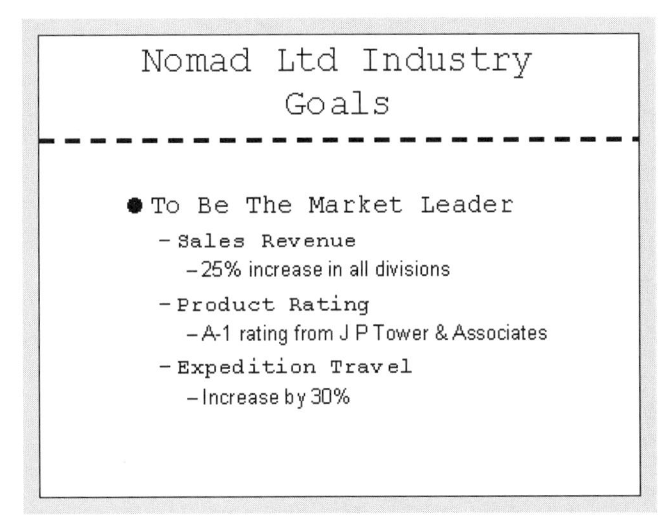

FIGURE 1-2: PowerPoint overhead

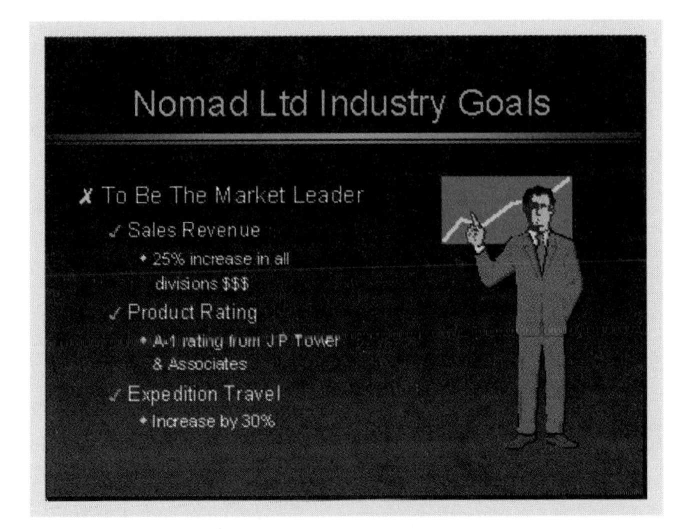

TABLE 1-1: PowerPoint output capabilities

OUTPUT	METHOD
35-mm slides	Use a film processing bureau to convert PowerPoint slides to 35-mm slides
B&W overheads	Print PowerPoint slides directly to transparencies on your B&W printer
Color overheads	Print PowerPoint slides directly to transparencies on your color printer
On-screen presentations	Run a slide show directly from your computer monitor or projector
Speaker notes	Print notes that help you remember points about each slide when you speak
Audience handouts	Print handouts with 2, 3, or 6 slides on a page
Outline pages	Print the outline of your presentation to show the main points

Starting PowerPoint 4.0 for Windows

To start PowerPoint, you first start Windows, as described in "Microsoft Windows 3.1." Then, you open the program group window that contains the PowerPoint application icon. This is usually the Microsoft Office program group, though your computer could have PowerPoint in its own program group. If you have trouble finding the program group that contains the PowerPoint application icon, check with your instructor or technical support person. If you are using a computer on a network, you might need to use a different starting procedure. You can also customize your starting procedure. See the related topic "Assigning a shortcut key to start PowerPoint" for more information. ▶ Lynn starts PowerPoint to familiarize herself with the application.

1 Make sure the Program Manager window is open

The Program Manager icon might appear at the bottom of your screen. Double-click it to open it, if necessary.

2 Double-click the **Microsoft Office program group icon**

The Microsoft Office program group window opens, displaying icons for PowerPoint and other Microsoft applications, as shown in Figure 1-3. Your screen might look different, depending on which applications are installed on your computer. If you cannot locate the Microsoft Office program group, click Window on the Program Manager menu bar, then click Microsoft Office.

3 Double-click the **Microsoft PowerPoint application icon**

PowerPoint opens. Unless a previous user has **disabled** (turned off) it, the Tip of the Day dialog box opens, as shown in Figure 1-4. This dialog box presents a new tip each time you start PowerPoint. The tips explain how to use PowerPoint features more effectively. If you don't want to see a tip every time you start PowerPoint, click the Show Tips at Startup check box to remove the "x" and turn the feature off. The rest of the book assumes you are familiar with the Tip of the Day dialog box.

4 If necessary, click **OK** to close Tip of the Day dialog box

The Tip of the Day dialog box closes, and the PowerPoint startup dialog box opens, allowing you to choose how you want to create your presentation. In the next lesson, Lynn chooses the AutoContent Wizard option in the PowerPoint startup dialog box to see how wizards can help her develop a presentation.

FIGURE 1-3: Microsoft Office program group

Microsoft PowerPoint application icon

List of available applications might vary

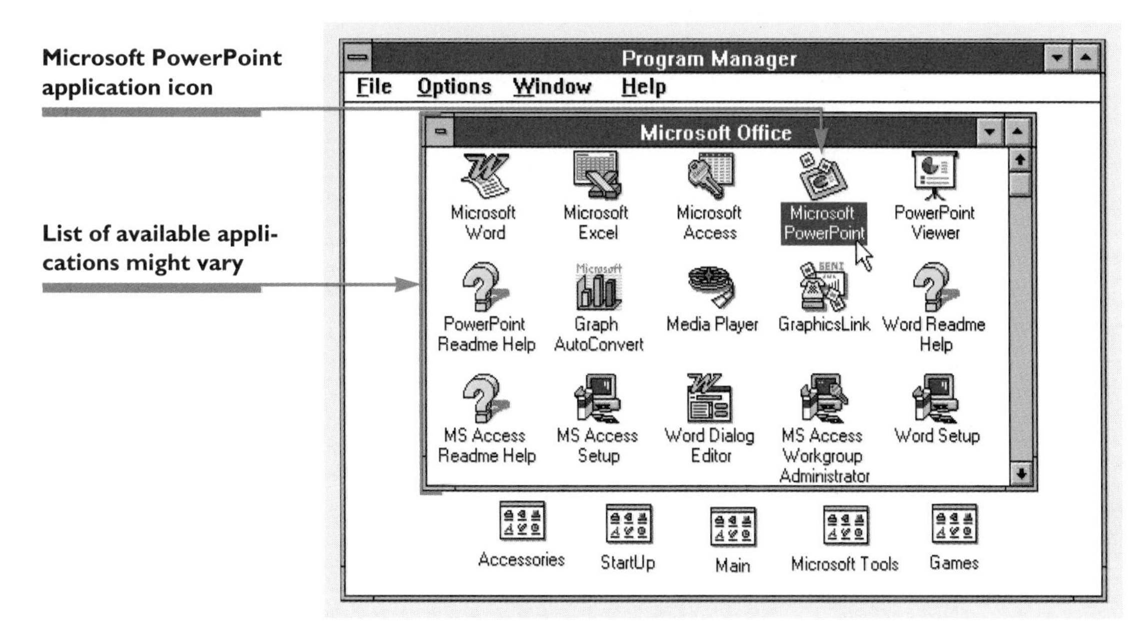

FIGURE 1-4: Tip of the Day dialog box

Indicates dialog box will open at startup

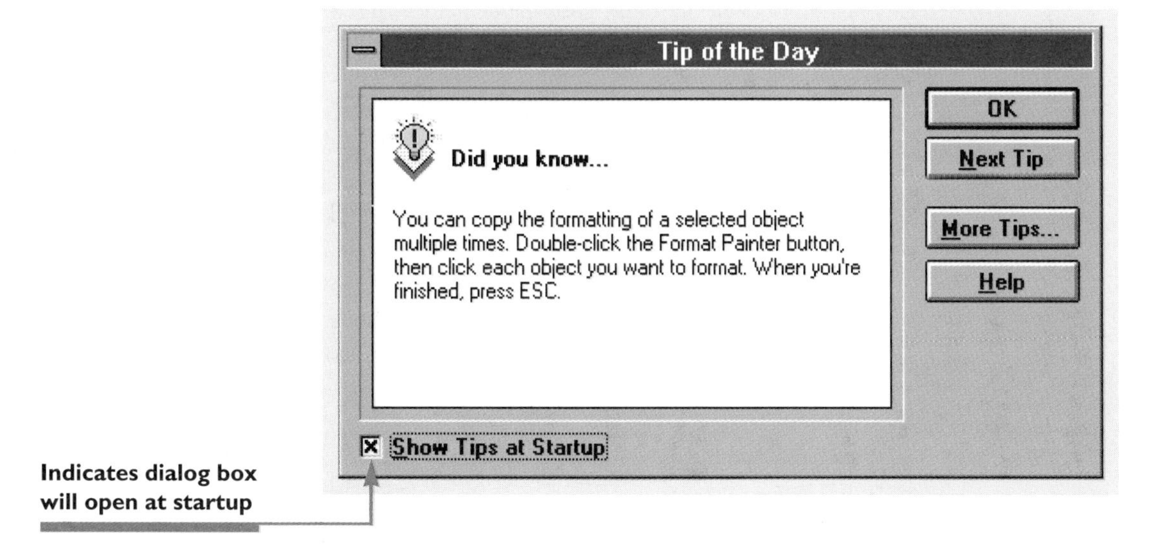

Assigning a shortcut key to start PowerPoint

To assign a shortcut key that starts PowerPoint automatically from the Program Manager, click the PowerPoint icon in Program Manager, click File on the menu bar, then click Properties. Click the Shortcut Key text box, press the keys you want to use, like [Ctrl] [Alt] [P], then click OK. You can then start PowerPoint without having to navigate a group window by simply pressing that key combination.

Using the AutoContent Wizard

The PowerPoint startup dialog box, shown in Figure 1-5, gives you five options for starting your presentation. The first option, the AutoContent Wizard, is the quickest way to create a presentation. A **wizard** is a series of steps that guides you through a task (in this case, creating a presentation). Using the AutoContent Wizard, you first create a title slide, then you choose a presentation category from the wizard's list of sample presentations. The AutoContent Wizard then creates an outline with sample text you can use as a guide to help formulate the major points of your presentation. See Table 1-2 for an explanation of all the options in the PowerPoint startup dialog box. ▶ Lynn continues to explore PowerPoint by opening the AutoContent Wizard.

1. **Click the AutoContent Wizard radio button, then click OK**
   The AutoContent Wizard opens and displays the Step 1 of 4 dialog box, which explains what the wizard is going to do.

2. **Click Next**
   The Step 2 of 4 dialog box opens, requesting information that will appear on the title slide of the presentation. Lynn types the title of her presentation in the first text box.

3. **Type Annual Report**
   The next two text boxes display information entered by the person who installed PowerPoint. Lynn enters the president's name and company name to complete the dialog box.

4. **Press [Tab] then type Bill Davidson; press [Tab], type Nomad Ltd, then click Next**
   The Step 3 of 4 dialog box opens, giving you six different presentation categories to choose from. Each presentation category generates a different sample outline. The president's presentation is going to be on the company's annual report so she chooses the Reporting Progress option.

5. **Click the Reporting Progress radio button**
   Notice that the sample outline in the view box on the left side of the dialog box changes to reflect the Reporting Progress category.

6. **Click Next, read the information in the dialog box, then click Finish**
   The AutoContent Wizard creates an outline with sample text based on the Reporting Progress category. Unless another user disabled it, PowerPoint displays **Cue Cards**, a step-by-step guide, on the right side of your window, as shown in Figure 1-6. See the related topic "Cue Cards" for more information. Lynn reads the information presented by Cue Cards, then closes the Cue Cards window in order to view her entire outline.

7. **If necessary, double-click the control menu box in the Cue Cards window to close it**
   The Cue Cards window closes, and the outline created by the AutoContent Wizard appears in full view.

FIGURE 1-5: PowerPoint startup dialog box

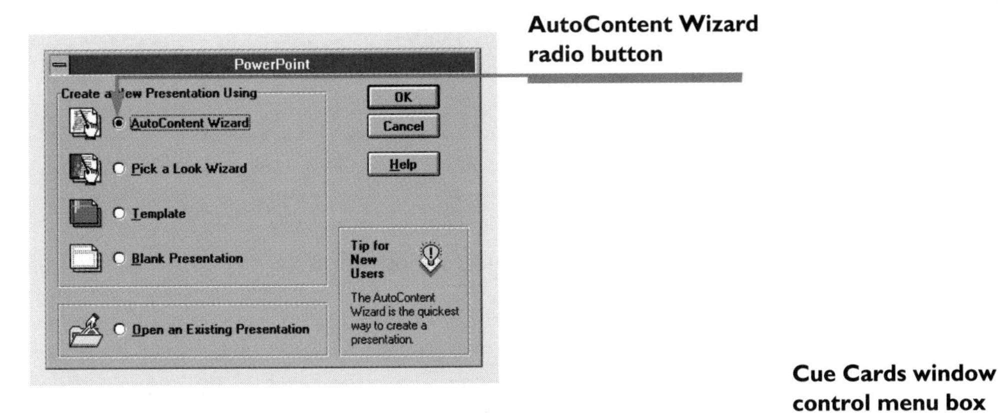

AutoContent Wizard radio button

FIGURE 1-6: Presentation window with Cue Cards window

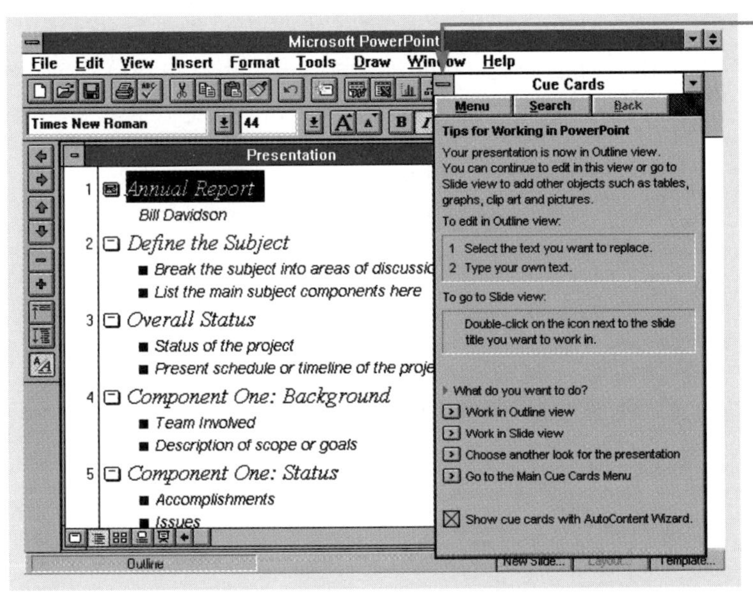

Cue Cards window control menu box

Cue Cards

PowerPoint Cue Cards walk you through simple and advanced tasks. You can open Cue Cards at any time by clicking Help on the menu bar, then clicking Cue Cards. The Cue Cards window stays on your screen while you perform the steps of the chosen task. Close the Cue Cards window by double-clicking its control menu box.

TABLE 1-2: PowerPoint startup dialog box options

OPTION	DESCRIPTION
AutoContent Wizard	Helps you determine the content and organization of your presentation by creating a title slide and outline using ready-made text for the category you choose
Pick a Look Wizard	Offers different visual formats to help you select a look and feel for your presentation
Template	Opens the Apply Template dialog box, displaying PowerPoint's preformatted templates
Blank Presentation	Opens the New Slide dialog box, allowing you to choose a predesigned slide layout
Open an Existing Presentation	Opens the File Open dialog box, allowing you to open a previously created presentation

Viewing the PowerPoint window

After you make your selection in the PowerPoint startup dialog box, the Presentation window appears within the PowerPoint window, displaying the presentation you just created or opened. You use the toolbars, buttons, and menu in the PowerPoint window to view and develop your presentation. PowerPoint has different **views** that allow you to see your presentation in different forms. You'll learn more about PowerPoint views in the next lesson. You move around in these views by using the scroll bars. See the related topic "Using the scroll bars" for more information. This lesson introduces you to elements of the PowerPoint window. Find and compare the elements described below using Figure 1-7. If you do not see a Presentation window as shown in Figure 1-7, see the Trouble? on the next page.

- The **title bar** displays the application name and contains a control menu box and resizing buttons, which you learned about in "Microsoft Windows 3.1."
- The **menu bar** lists the names of the menus you use to choose PowerPoint commands. Clicking a menu name on the menu bar displays a list of commands from which you might choose.
- The **Standard toolbar** contains buttons for the most frequently used commands, such as copying and pasting. Clicking buttons on a toolbar is often faster than using the menu. However, in some cases, using the menu offers additional options not available by clicking a button.
- The **Formatting toolbar** contains buttons for the most frequently used commands, such as changing font type and size.
- The **Outlining toolbar** appears only in Outline view, the current view. The Outlining toolbar contains buttons for the most frequently used outlining commands, such as moving and indenting text lines.
- The **Presentation window** is the "canvas" where you type text, work with lines and shapes, and view your presentation.
- The **status bar**, located at the bottom of the PowerPoint window, displays messages about what you are doing and seeing in PowerPoint.

FIGURE 1-7: PowerPoint window in Outline view

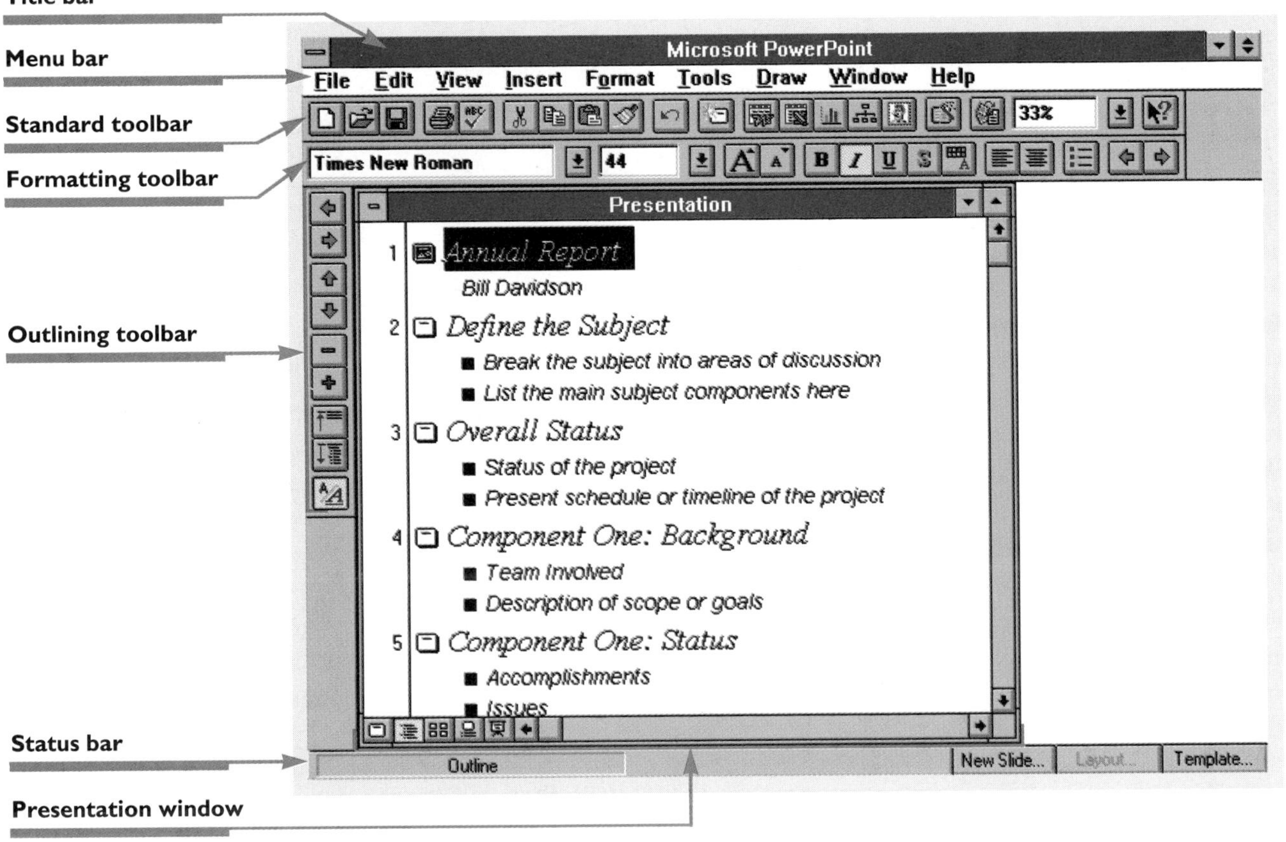

Title bar

Menu bar

Standard toolbar

Formatting toolbar

Outlining toolbar

Status bar

Presentation window

Using the scroll bars

Sometimes you need to **scroll**, or move, within a window to see more of the window contents. There are three ways to scroll in PowerPoint: click the vertical scroll arrows to move one line at a time; click above or below the vertical scroll box to move one screen at a time; or drag the vertical scroll box to move quickly to any point in the window. The scroll box for the vertical scroll bar is called the **elevator**. Use the horizontal scroll bar to move the screen to the left or the right.

TROUBLE?

If your PowerPoint window doesn't look similar to Figure 1-7, your Presentation window might be maximized to fill the entire PowerPoint window. Click the lower Restore button to return the Presentation window to its original size. Size it to look like Figure 1-7, if necessary.

Viewing your presentation

This lesson introduces you to PowerPoint's five views: Outline view, Slide view, Notes Pages view, Slide Sorter view, and Slide Show view. Each PowerPoint view displays your presentation in a different way and allows you to manipulate your presentation differently. See Table 1-3 for a brief description of the PowerPoint view buttons. To easily move between the PowerPoint views, you use view buttons located at the bottom of the Presentation window, as shown in Figure 1-8. ▶ Follow Lynn as she moves between each PowerPoint view.

1 Click the **down scroll arrow** repeatedly to scroll through your presentation outline

As you scroll through the presentation, notice that each of the nine slides in the presentation is identified by a number along the left side of the outline.

2 Click the **Slide View button** on the status bar

PowerPoint switches to Slide view and displays the first slide in the presentation, which corresponds to the slide title and main point on the first slide in Outline view. To see what some of her slides look like, Lynn decides to scroll through her presentation by dragging the elevator.

3 Drag the elevator down the vertical scroll bar until the Slide Indicator box, which appears, displays Slide 3, then release the mouse button

The **Slide Indicator box** tells you which slide will appear when you release the mouse button, as shown in Figure 1-9. To return to Slide 1, Lynn uses the Previous Slide button instead of the elevator.

4 Click the **Previous Slide button** twice to move back to Slide 1

The elevator moves back up the scroll bar, and PowerPoint returns Lynn to Slide 1.

5 Click the **Notes Pages View button**

Slide view changes to Notes Pages view, showing you a reduced image of the title slide above a large box. Lynn can enter text in this box and then print the notes page to help her remember important points of her presentation.

6 Click the **Slide Sorter View button**

A miniature image of each slide in the presentation appears in this view. Lynn can examine the flow of her slides and easily move them if they need to be rearranged.

7 Click the **Slide Show button**

The first slide fills the entire screen. In this view, Lynn can practice running through her slides and set special effects so the presentation can be shown as an electronic slide show.

8 Click the **left mouse button** to advance through the slides one at a time until you return to Slide Sorter view.

FIGURE 1-8: Outline view

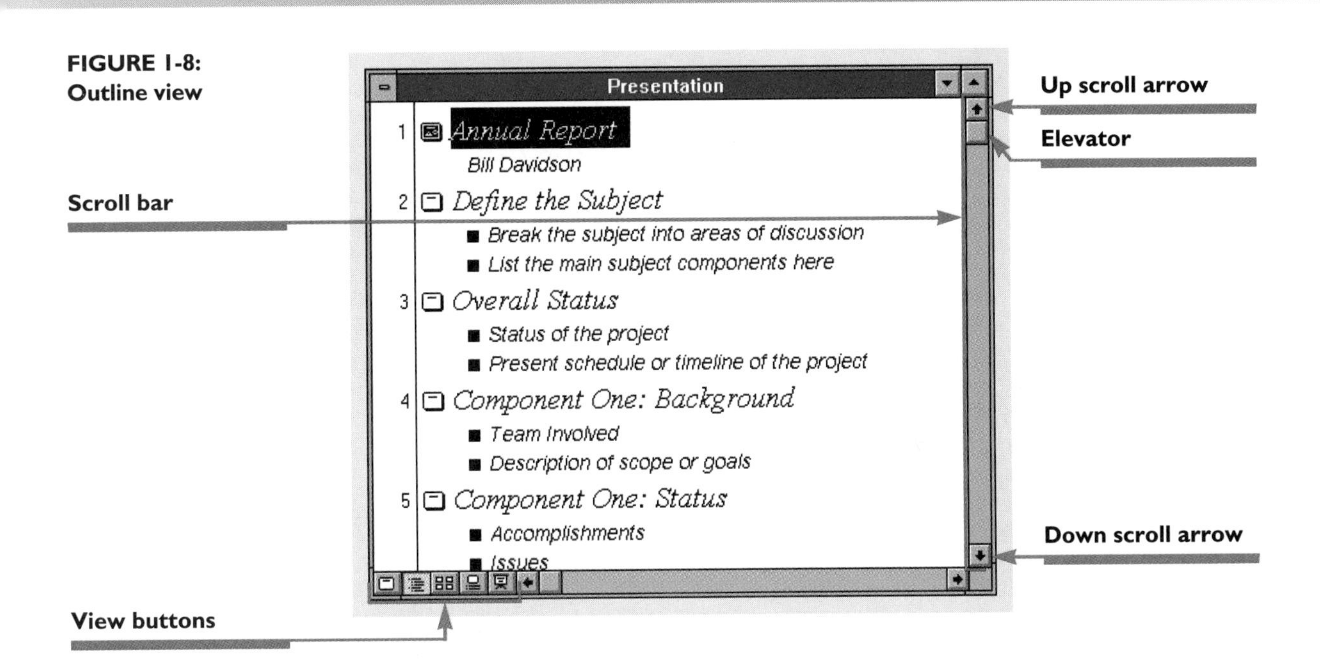

FIGURE 1-9: Slide view

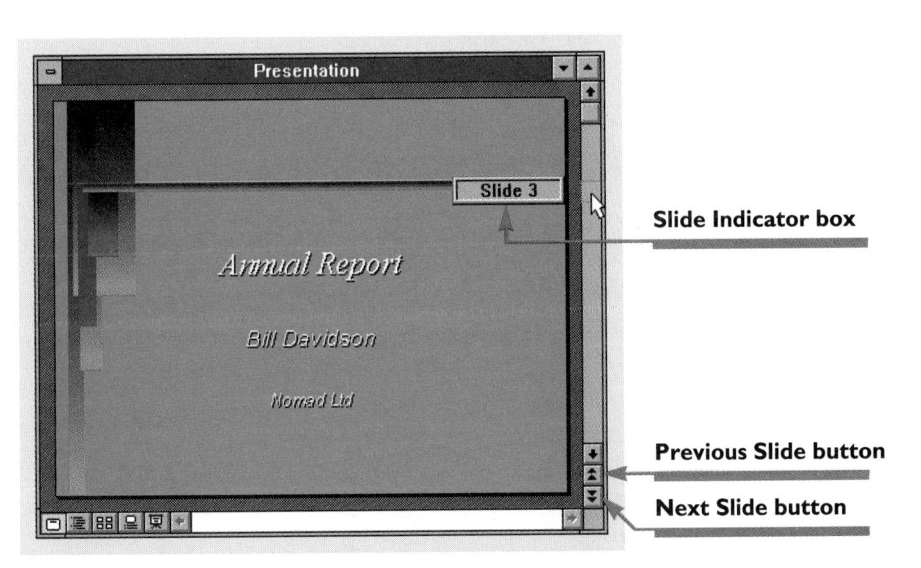

TABLE 1-3: View buttons

BUTTON	BUTTON NAME	DESCRIPTION
	Outline View	Displays the title and main topics in the form of an outline. Use this view to enter and edit the text of your presentation.
	Slide View	Displays one slide at a time. Use this view to modify and enhance a slide's appearance.
	Notes Pages View	Displays a reduced slide image and a box to type notes. Use this view to take notes on your slides, which you can use during your presentation.
	Slide Sorter View	Displays a miniature picture of each slide in the order they appear in your presentation. Use this view to rearrange and add special effects to your slides.
	Slide Show	Displays your presentation as an electronic slide show.

Working with toolbars

The PowerPoint toolbars offer easy access to commonly used commands. Each PowerPoint view displays different toolbars containing toolbar buttons appropriate for the tasks you perform in that view. You can place the toolbars anywhere on your screen or remove them, depending on your needs. If you have a small monitor, you might want to remove a toolbar so you can see more of your presentation. See the related topic "Arranging toolbars" for more information. PowerPoint has eight ready-made toolbars that you can add, remove, or modify at any time. ▶ In this lesson, Lynn uses the Formatting toolbar to format a slide title.

1. Click the **Outline View button**
   The outline fills the Presentation window with the first slide title selected. In Outline view, text such as the slide title must be selected before you move or change it. Lynn decides to change the title slide font attributes (the appearance of the typeface) from italic to bold italic.

2. On the Formatting toolbar, move the mouse pointer over the Bold button *but do not click*
   The Formatting toolbar appears below the Standard toolbar, as shown in Figure 1-10. Notice that as the mouse pointer rests over the Bold button, a small box, called a **ToolTip**, appears, identifying the Bold button.

3. Move the mouse pointer over other toolbar buttons on the Formatting toolbar to display their ToolTips
   Notice that a brief description of the button also appears in the status bar. ToolTips also appear for the view buttons and the Next and Previous Slide buttons.

4. Click on the Formatting toolbar
   PowerPoint bolds the slide title, Annual Report. The Bold button is a **toggle button**, which you click to turn the bold attribute on or off. Now that the title is bold, Lynn decides to increase its font size so it is more visible.

5. Click the **Increase Font Size button** on the Formatting toolbar
   The font size for the title increases from 44 to 48. The Font Size list box displays the font size change.

FIGURE 1-10: PowerPoint window showing ToolTip

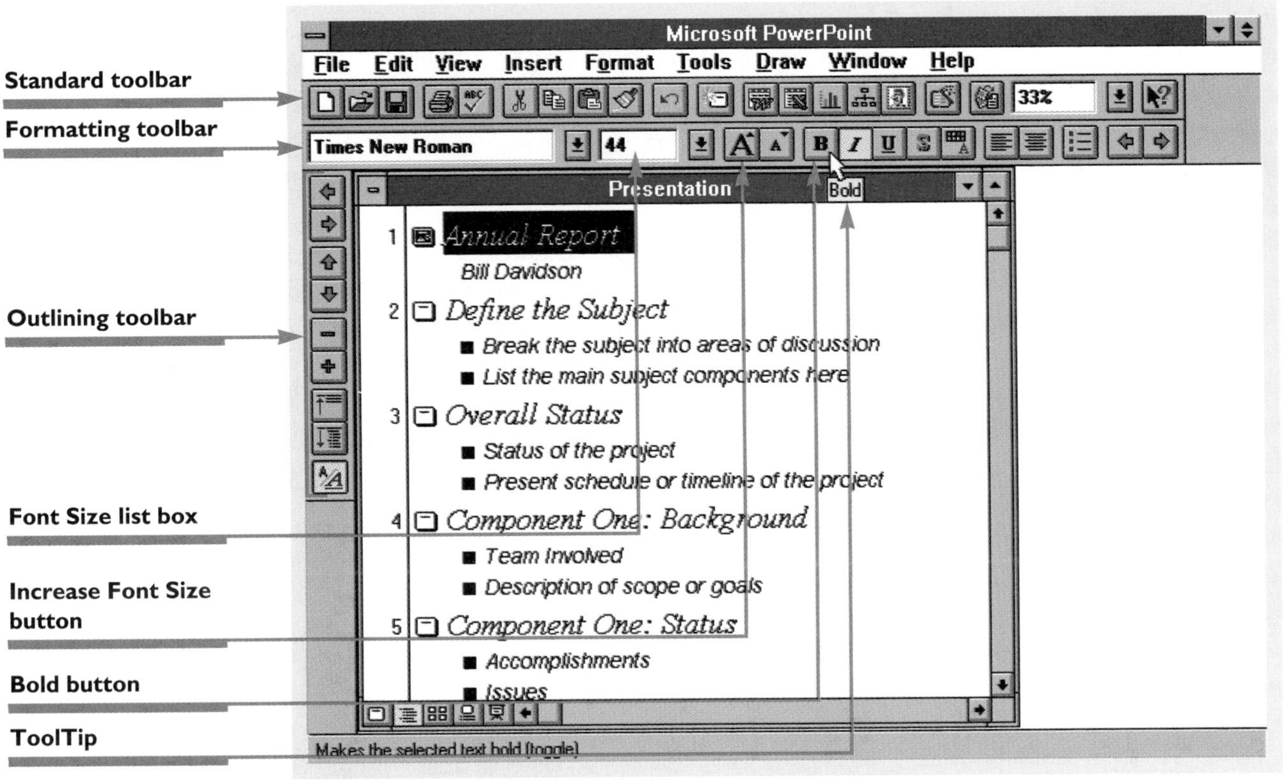

Standard toolbar

Formatting toolbar

Outlining toolbar

Font Size list box

Increase Font Size button

Bold button

ToolTip

Arranging toolbars

You can move or hide PowerPoint toolbars at any time. Move a toolbar by clicking an open space on the toolbar and dragging it to a new location. An outline of the toolbar appears so you can see how the toolbar will look when you release the mouse button. You can hide a toolbar by double-clicking its control menu box.

You can add or delete toolbar buttons using the Customize command from the Tools menu.

Getting Help

PowerPoint has an extensive on-line Help system that gives you immediate access to definitions, reference information, and feature explanations. Help information appears in a separate window that you can move and resize. ▶ Lynn likes the flexibility of the toolbars and decides to find out more about them.

1 **Click Help on the menu bar, then click Search for Help on**
The PowerPoint Help window opens displaying the Search dialog box. Lynn decides to use the Search dialog box to find out more about toolbars.

2 Type **toolbar** in the search text box containing the blinking insertion point
Notice that as you type each character in this text box, the list of topics scrolls. The list box displays three toolbar categories: toolbar buttons, toolbar commands, and toolbars.

3 Click **toolbars** in the list box, then click **Show Topics**
Help displays all the toolbar-related topics in the lower list box, as shown in Figure 1-11. To view all the topics in this box, click the down scroll arrow.

4 Click **Adding buttons to toolbars** in the lower list box, then click **Go To**
The Search dialog box closes. The Help window displays the steps to add buttons to toolbars, as shown in Figure 1-12. Your Help window might look different than Figure 1-12, so use the scroll arrows to move up and down the Help window to view all the information, if necessary. Refer to Table 1-4 for a description of the available Help buttons.

5 If necessary, click the **down scroll arrow** in the Help window until the "See also" section appears

6 Click **The Toolbars** when the pointer changes to
Related information on toolbars appears in the Help window. Lynn reads this information and decides to close the Help window.

7 Double-click the **control menu box** in the Help window to close it
The Help window closes and you return to your presentation.

TABLE 1-4:
The Help buttons

BUTTON	DESCRIPTION
Contents	Displays Help topic categories
Search	Opens a dialog box where you specify a topic you want help with
Back	Returns you to the previous topic
History	Shows you a list of the Help topics to which you have referred
<<	Moves to the previous Help topic
>>	Moves to the next Help topic

FIGURE 1-11: Search dialog box

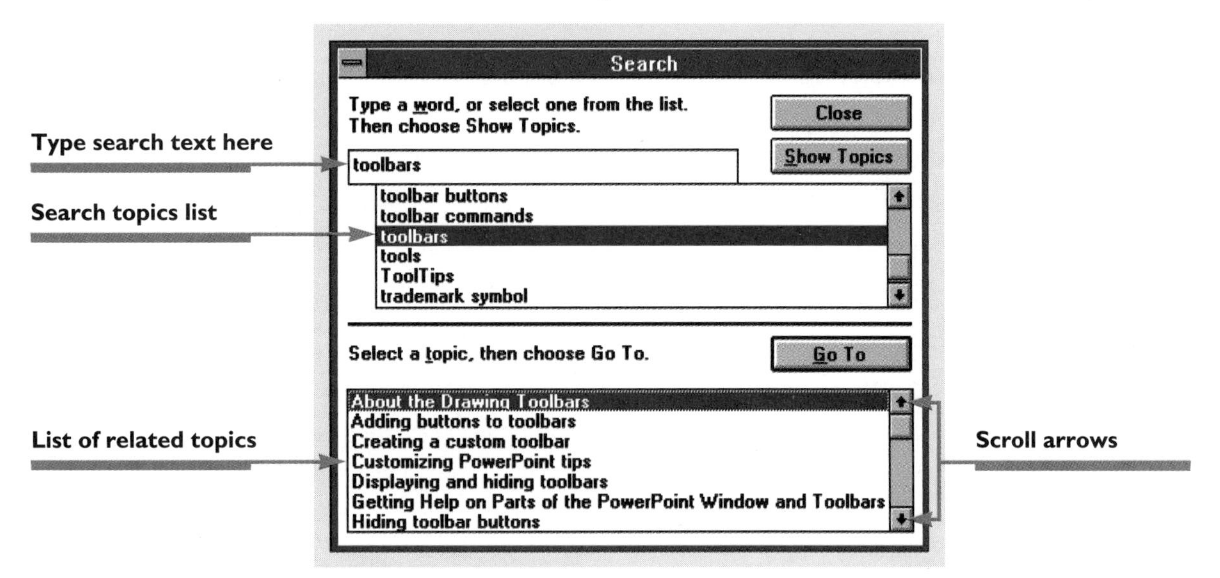

FIGURE 1-12: Help window

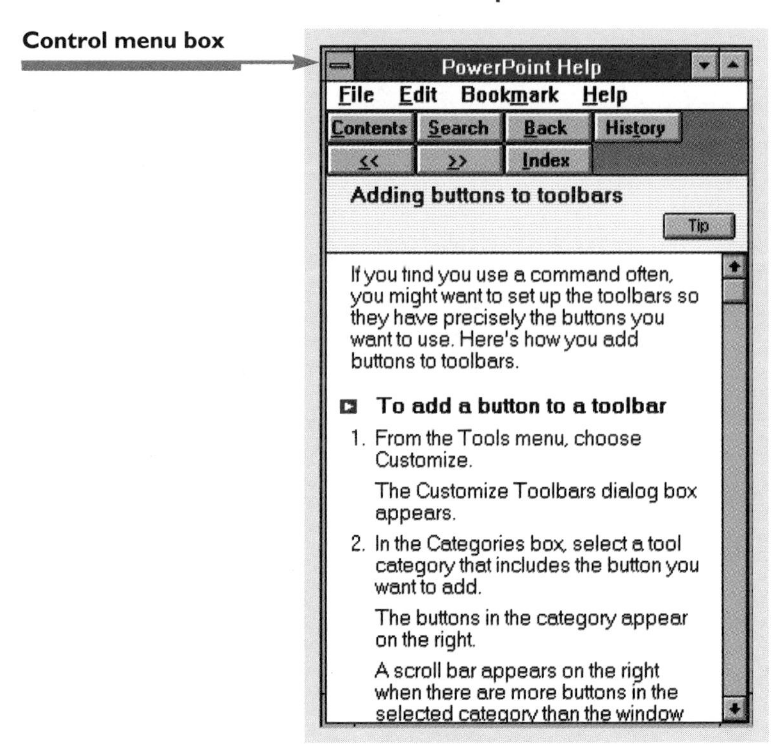

QUICK TIP

On the Standard toolbar, click the Help button and then click a window item to jump to the Help topic for that item.

Closing a file and exiting PowerPoint

When you finish working on your presentation, you generally save your work and then close the file containing your presentation. When you are done using PowerPoint, you need to exit the program. For a comparison of the Close and Exit commands, refer to Table 1-5. ▶ Lynn needs to go to a meeting, so she exits PowerPoint without saving the file. She can easily re-create this presentation later and use it as the basis of her annual report if she so chooses.

1. **Click File on the menu bar, then click Close, as shown in Figure 1-13**
   A Microsoft PowerPoint dialog box opens, as shown in Figure 1-14, asking you to save your presentation. Because Lynn was just exploring PowerPoint features, she does not want to save this presentation.
2. **Click No**
   The Presentation window closes.
3. **Click File on the menu bar, then click Exit**
   The PowerPoint application closes, and you return to the Program Manager.

If you want to exit PowerPoint without saving your work and closing the presentation, click File on the menu bar, click Exit, then click No when asked if you want to save your changes.

TABLE 1-5: Understanding the Close and Exit commands

CLOSING A FILE	EXITING POWERPOINT
Puts a file away	Puts all files away
Leaves PowerPoint loaded in computer memory	Frees computer memory up for other uses

FIGURE 1-13: File menu

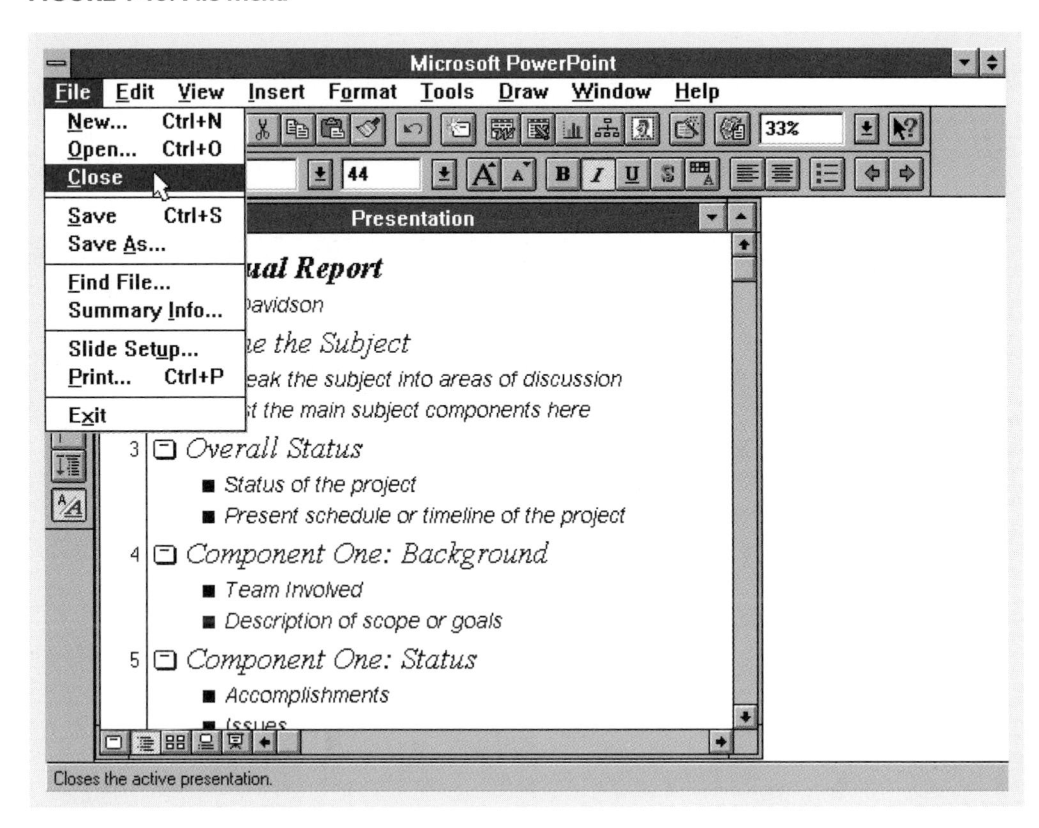

FIGURE 1-14: Microsoft PowerPoint dialog box

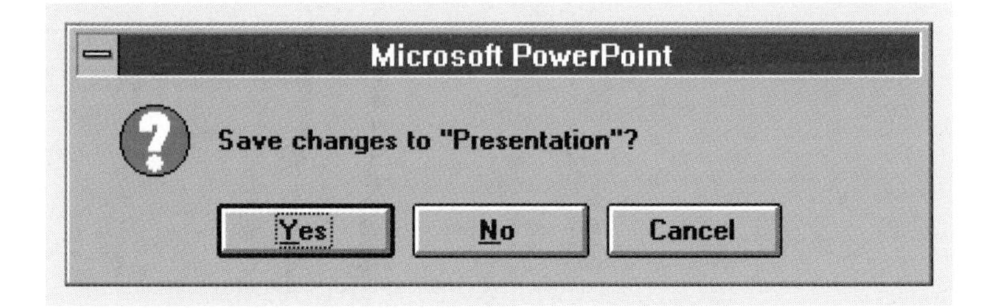

QUICK TIP

Double-clicking the control menu box next to the menu bar closes the presentation. Double-clicking the control menu box in the title bar exits the application.

CONCEPTSREVIEW

Label the PowerPoint window elements shown in Figure 1-15.

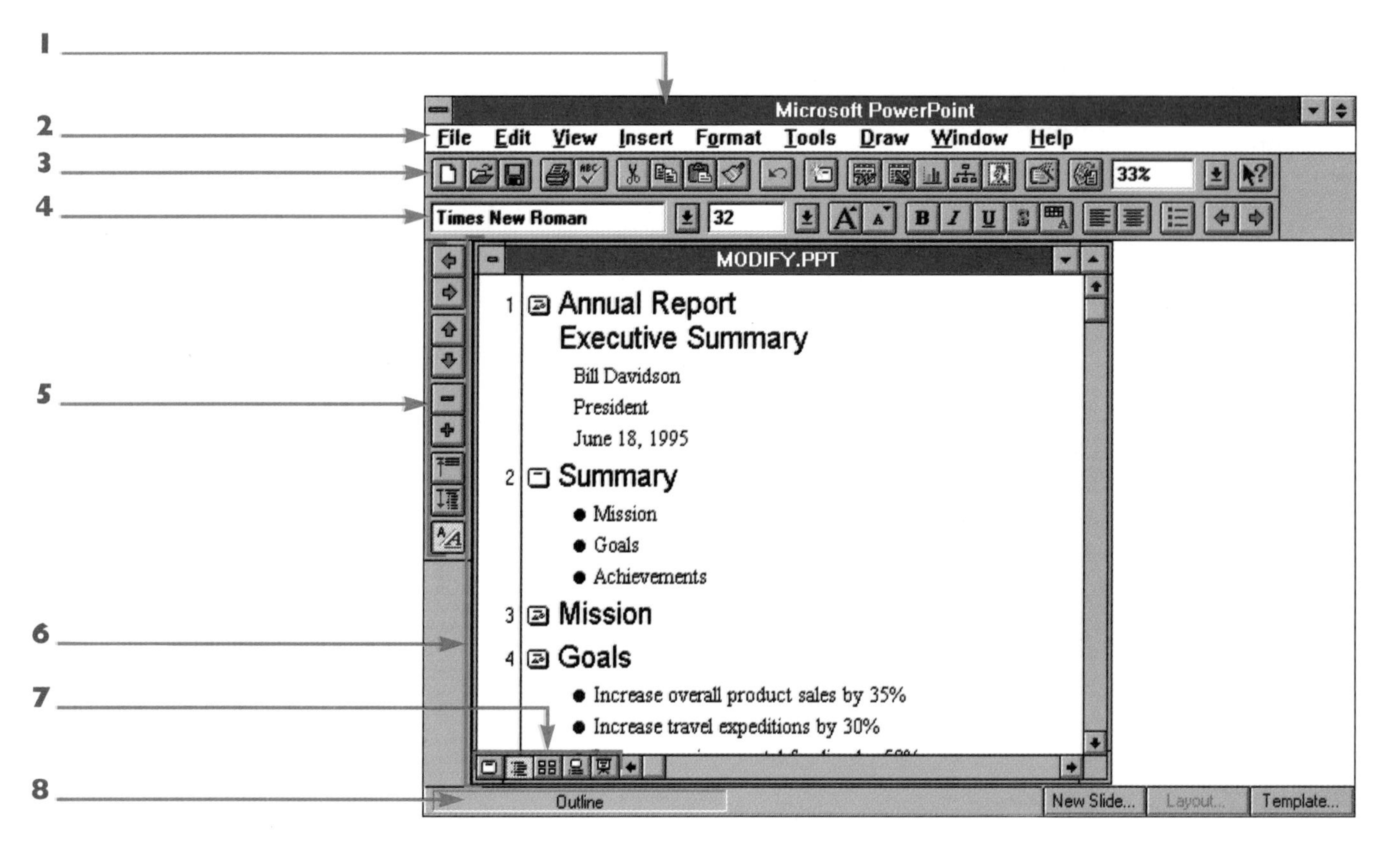

FIGURE 1-15

Match each term with the statement that describes its function.

9 The area where you work on your presentation

10 An on-screen step-by-step guide

11 Small box that identifies a tool button

12 Dialog box that contains PowerPoint hints

13 Small box in the vertical scroll bar

a. ToolTip
b. Tip of the Day
c. Presentation window
d. Elevator
e. Cue Cards

Select the best answer from the list of choices.

14 PowerPoint can help you create all of the following, EXCEPT:
a. 35-mm slides
b. Movies
c. An on-screen presentation
d. Outline pages

15 The buttons that you use to switch between the PowerPoint views are called
a. PowerPoint buttons
b. View buttons
c. Screen buttons
d. Toolbar buttons

16 All of these are PowerPoint views, EXCEPT:

a. Slide view

b. Notes Pages view

c. Outline view

d. Current Page view

17 The term for moving to different parts of your slide or outline is

a. Scrolling

b. Aligning

c. Moving

d. Shifting

18 This view shows your presentation electronically:

a. Electronic view

b. Slide Sorter view

c. Presentation view

d. Slide Show view

19 Which wizard helps you organize and outline your presentation?

a. Pick a Look Wizard

b. Presentation Wizard

c. AutoContent Wizard

d. OrgContent Wizard

APPLICATIONS REVIEW

1 Start PowerPoint and use the AutoContent Wizard to create a sample presentation on a topic of your choice.

a. Double-click the PowerPoint application icon in the Microsoft Office program group window.

b. Click the AutoContent Wizard radio button, then click OK.

c. Fill in the necessary information in the Step 2 of 4 dialog box.

d. Choose a presentation category in the Step 3 of 4 dialog box, then click Finish.

2 Work with Cue Cards and view the PowerPoint window.

a. If necessary, click Cue Cards on the Help menu. Click one of the menu buttons located at the bottom of the Cue Cards window.

b. Read through the Cue Card steps at the top of the window on the subject you chose.

c. Double-click the control menu box on the Cue Cards window to close it.

d. Your outline is in full view. Examine the content of the sample outline.

e. Identify as many elements of the PowerPoint window as you can without referring to the unit material.

3 Explore the PowerPoint views.

a. Use the scroll arrows to move up and down the outline to view its content.

b. Click the Slide View button. Notice that a description of the view button appears in the status bar.

c. Click the Next Slide button to view your slides.

d. Click the Notes Pages View button, and drag the elevator up and down to view your notes pages. After you finish exploring, drag the elevator to slide.

e. Click the Slide Sorter View button, and examine your slides.

f. Click the Slide Show button. The first slide of your presentation fills the screen. Advance through the slide show by clicking the left mouse button.

4 Explore the PowerPoint toolbars.

a. Click the Outline View button.

b. Click the Increase Font Size button.

c. Click the Underline button to underline the title.

5 Explore PowerPoint Help.

a. Click Help on the menu bar, then click Contents. The Help window opens.

b. Click the Reference Information icon.

c. Click Getting Help on Menu Commands and read the Help information on menu commands.

d. Double-click the control menu box to close the Contents window.

e. Double-click the control menu box to close the PowerPoint Help window.

6 Close your presentation and exit PowerPoint.

a. Click File on the menu bar, then click Close.

b. Click No if you see a message asking if you want to save the changes.

c. Click File on the menu bar, then click Exit.

INDEPENDENT CHALLENGE 1

PowerPoint offers an interactive tutorial called Quick Preview, which gives you an overview of PowerPoint's features. The Quick Preview covers the PowerPoint Wizards, adding a new slide, and adding graphs, tables, templates, and clip art. To work through the Quick Preview, click Help on the menu bar, then click Quick Preview. Click the appropriate buttons to proceed through the preview, and then click Quit when you are finished.

INDEPENDENT CHALLENGE 2

You are in charge of marketing for AllSigns, Inc., a medium size company that produces all types of business and professional signs. The company has a regional sales area that includes three neighboring Northeast states. You found out today that AllSigns' president just confirmed a deal with American Hotels, a national hotel chain, to present a proposal for a large contract to make signs for all of their hotels.

Because you are in charge of marketing, you are given the responsibility of planning and creating the outline of the proposal the president will present to American Hotels.

Create an outline that reflects the major issues AllSigns needs to convey to American Hotels to secure a large contract. Assume the following: AllSigns needs to promote their company and products to American Hotels; AllSigns make all types of signs from outdoor advertising signs to indoor informational and directional signs; the AllSigns proposal includes outdoor advertising signs and indoor informational signs.

To complete this independent challenge:

1. Use the AutoContent Wizard to help you create a promotional outline.
2. Plan how you would change and add to the sample text created by the wizard. What information do you need to promote AllSigns to a large company?
3. Take notes on how you might change the outline text. In the next unit, you'll learn how to enter your own text into a presentation.

UNIT 2

OBJECTIVES

- Plan an effective presentation
- Choose a look for a presentation
- Enter slide text
- Create a new slide
- Work in Outline view
- Enter text in Notes Pages view
- Save a presentation
- Print a presentation

Creating A PRESENTATION

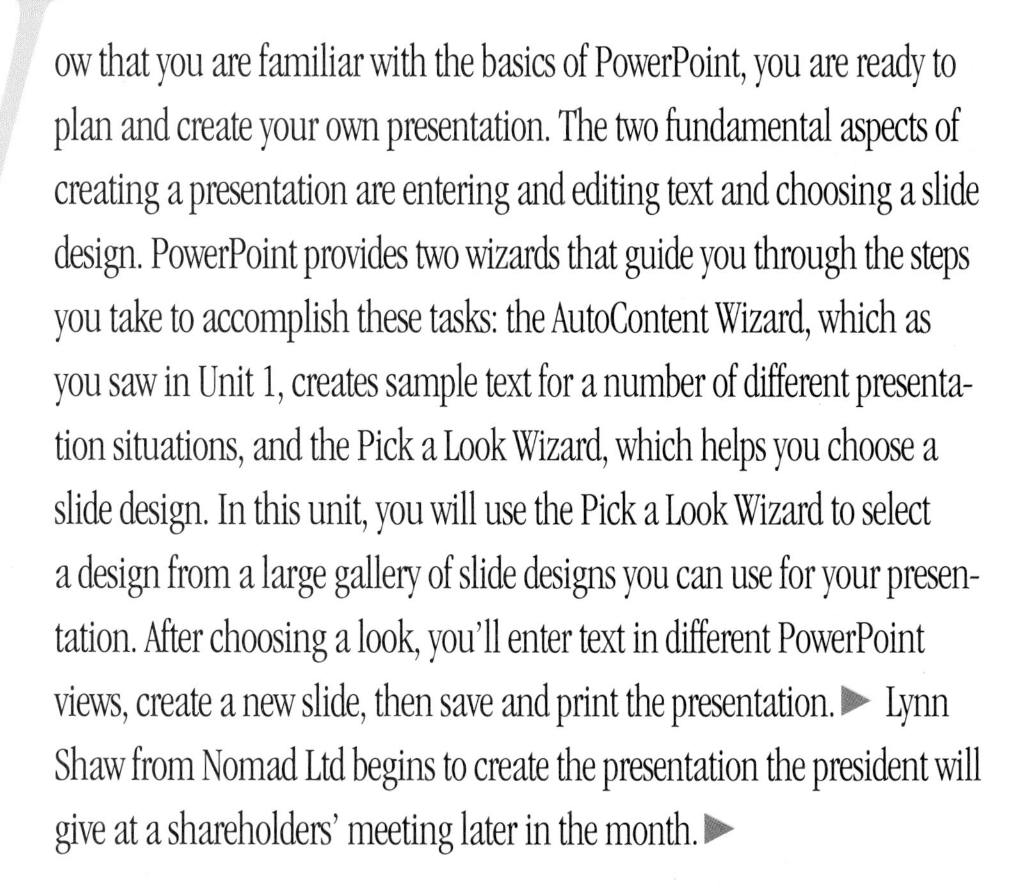

Now that you are familiar with the basics of PowerPoint, you are ready to plan and create your own presentation. The two fundamental aspects of creating a presentation are entering and editing text and choosing a slide design. PowerPoint provides two wizards that guide you through the steps you take to accomplish these tasks: the AutoContent Wizard, which as you saw in Unit 1, creates sample text for a number of different presentation situations, and the Pick a Look Wizard, which helps you choose a slide design. In this unit, you will use the Pick a Look Wizard to select a design from a large gallery of slide designs you can use for your presentation. After choosing a look, you'll enter text in different PowerPoint views, create a new slide, then save and print the presentation. ▶ Lynn Shaw from Nomad Ltd begins to create the presentation the president will give at a shareholders' meeting later in the month. ▶

Planning an effective presentation

Before you begin a presentation, you need to plan and outline the message you want to communicate and consider how you want it to look. In preparing the outline, you need to consider where you are giving the presentation and who your primary audience is going to be. It's also important to know what resources you might need, such as a computer or projection equipment. ▶ Using Figure 2-1 and Figure 2-2 and the planning guidelines below, follow Lynn as she outlines the presentation message.

1. **Determine the purpose of the presentation and the location and audience.**
   The president needs to present the highlights of Nomad's Annual Report at a shareholders' meeting at the Plaza Center Inn in a large hall.

2. **Determine the type of output, either black and white (B&W) or color overhead transparencies, on-screen slide show, or 35-mm slides, that best conveys your message, given time constraints and hardware availability.**
   Since the president is speaking in a large hall and has access to a computer and projection equipment, Lynn decides to produce an on-screen slide show.

3. **Determine a look for your presentation that will help communicate your message. You can choose a professionally designed template quickly and easily with PowerPoint's Pick a Look Wizard.**
   Lynn needs to choose a template that will appeal to the audience and help reinforce a message of confidence and accomplishment.

4. **Determine the message you want to communicate. Give the presentation a meaningful title and then outline your message and organize your thoughts.**
   Lynn titles the presentation "Annual Report Executive Summary" and then outlines the message with the information given her by the president, who wants to highlight the previous year's accomplishments and set the goals for the coming year (Figure 2-1).

5. **Determine what you want to produce when the presentation is finished. You need to prepare not only the slides themselves, but supplementary materials, including notes for the speaker, handouts for the audience, and an outline of the presentation.**
   Lynn knows the president wants speaker's notes to refer to during his presentation. Speaker's notes allow the president to stay on track and deliver a concise message.

6. **Roughly sketch on paper how you want the slides and words on the slides to look. Use this sketch to help guide your choices as you progress through the Pick a Look Wizard.**
   Lynn wants a bold and bright look to convey a sense of accomplishment and excitement. Her sketch looks like Figure 2-2.

FIGURE 2-1: Outline of text for presentation

1. Annual Report Executive Summary
   — Bill Davidson
   — June 18, 1995

2. Summary
   — Goals
   — Accomplishments

3. Goals
   — Product sales up 35%
   — Travel expeditions up 30%
   — Environmental funding up 50%

4. Accomplishments
   — Product sales up 53.4%
   — Travel expeditions up 26.9%
   — Environmental funding up 5.4%

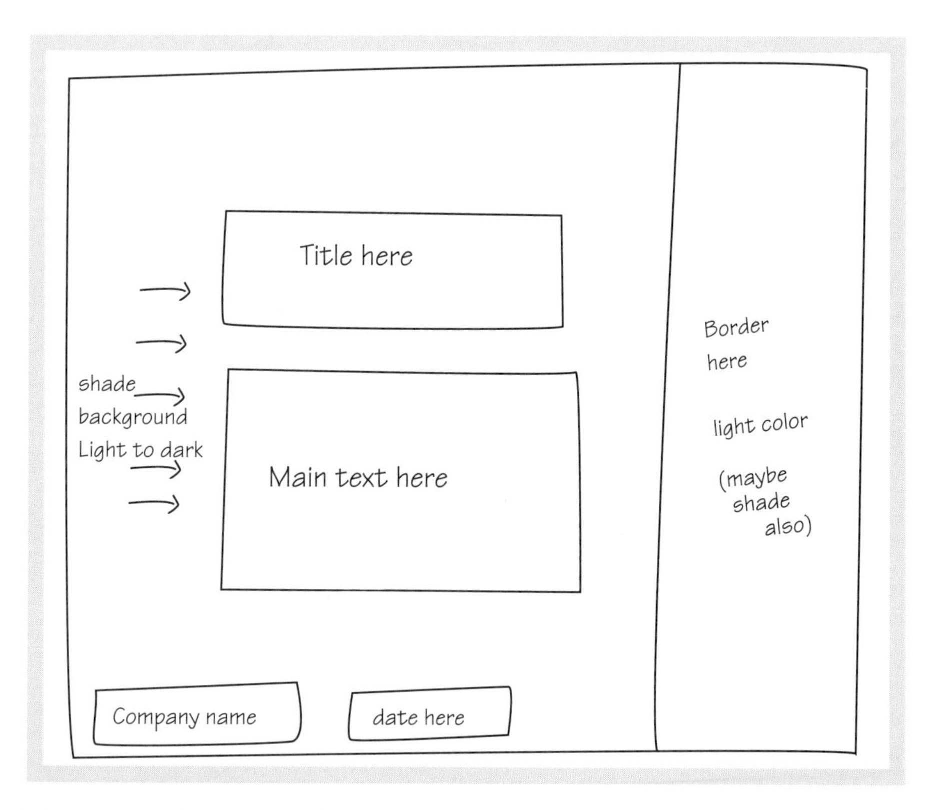

FIGURE 2-2: Presentation slide design sketch

Choosing a look for a presentation

With PowerPoint's Pick a Look Wizard, you don't have to be an artist or spend hours to create a great looking presentation. The **Pick a Look Wizard** is a series of steps that leads you through choosing a look for your presentation. The PowerPoint software comes with a collection of prepared slide designs that have borders, colors, text attributes, and other elements arranged in a variety of formats. You can also create your own design if you have time. ▶ Lynn doesn't have a lot of time but wants to create a good-looking presentation, so she uses the Pick a Look Wizard to help her choose the slide design for the president's presentation.

1. Start PowerPoint, click the **Pick a Look Wizard radio button** in the PowerPoint startup dialog box, then click **OK**
   The Pick a Look Wizard opens and displays the Step 1 of 9 dialog box, which explains what the Wizard is going to do.
2. Click **Next**
   The Step 2 of 9 dialog box opens, giving you four different output options that determine the color and style of your presentation. Lynn decides to develop the presentation on a white background and add the color and shading later so she chooses the Color Overheads option.
3. Click the **Color Overheads radio button**, then click **Next**
   The Step 3 of 9 dialog box opens, as shown in Figure 2-3, giving you a choice of four slide background designs, called **templates**. To view additional templates, click the More button.
4. Click **More**, click the **File Name down scroll arrow** until the SOARINGC.PPT template appears, then click **SOARINGC.PPT**
   A sample of the SOARINGC.PPT template appears in the Preview box. See Figure 2-4.
5. Click **Apply** then click **Next**
6. Click the **Audience Handout Pages check box** and click the **Outline Pages check box** to deselect them, then click **Next**
   The Slide Options dialog box gives you three options that you can place on every slide: Name, Date, and Page Number. Lynn decides to include the company name and the date on the slides.
7. If necessary, highlight the text in the text box below the Name, company, or other text check box, then type **Nomad Ltd** to replace it
8. Click the **Date check box**, then click **Next**
   For the speaker's notes, Lynn just wants the page number, selected by default.
9. Click **Next**, read the information in the dialog box, then click **Finish**
   The Pick a Look Wizard closes and creates a title slide with the presentation design you selected, shown in Slide view with the Drawing toolbar available. The special characters (//) on the bottom of the slide indicate where PowerPoint will print the current date. See Figure 2-5.

FIGURE 2-3: Pick a Look Wizard - Step 3 of 9 dialog box

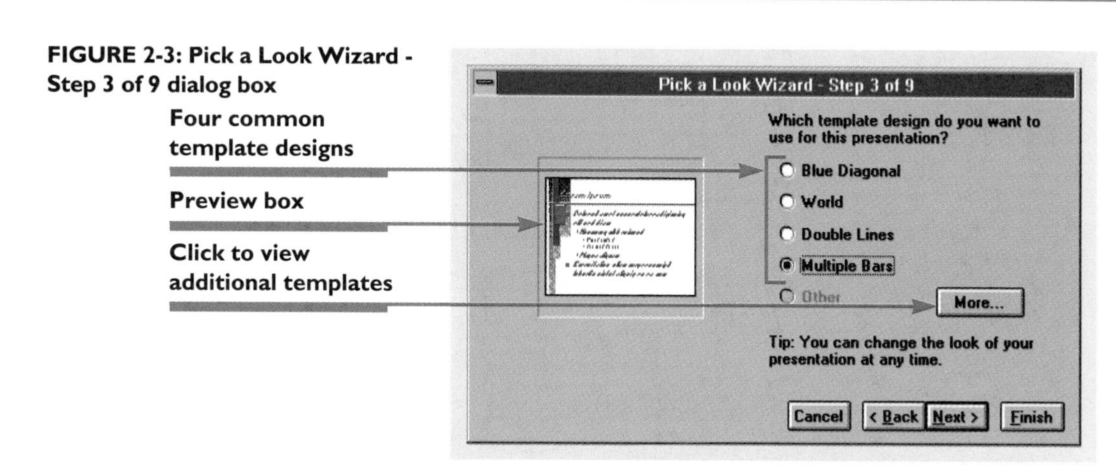

FIGURE 2-4: Presentation Template dialog box

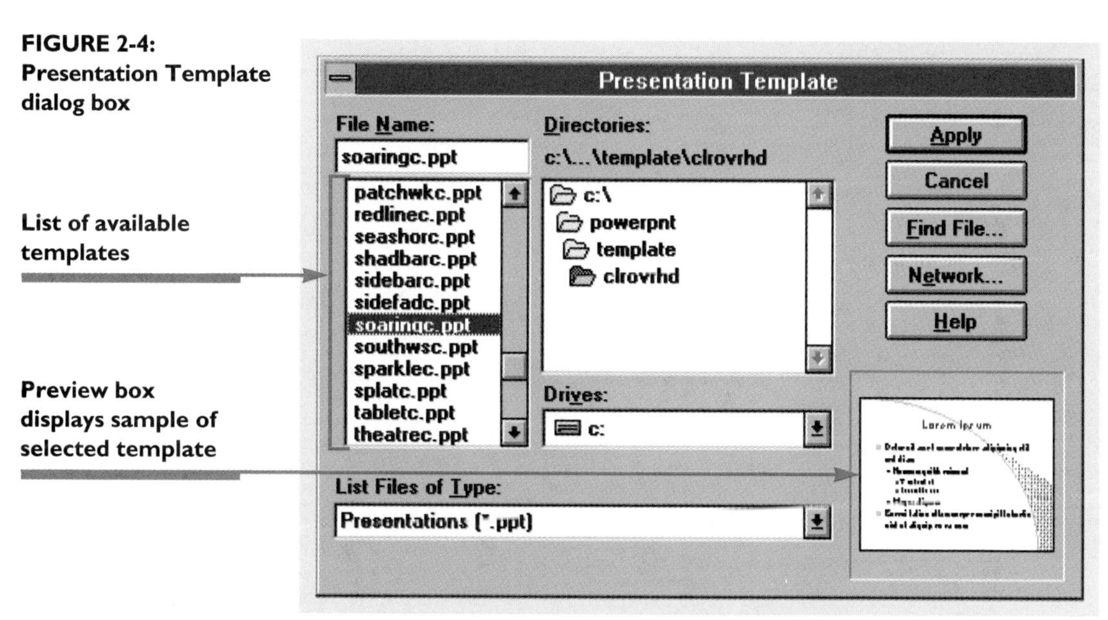

FIGURE 2-5: Presentation title slide

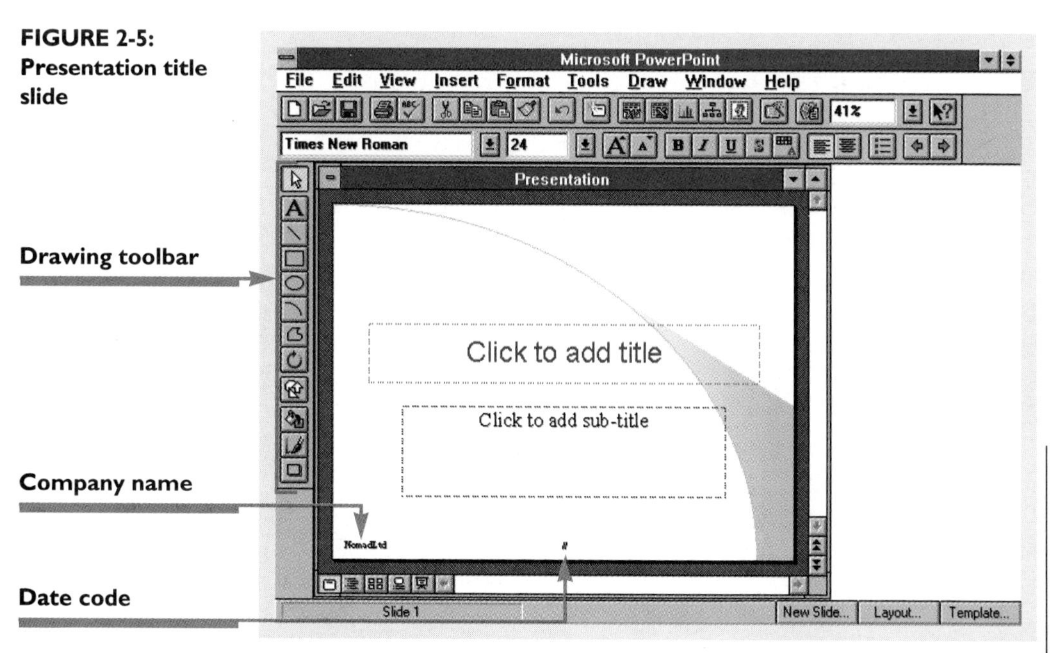

TROUBLE?

If you need help starting PowerPoint, refer to the lesson "Starting PowerPoint 4.0 for Windows" in Unit 1.

Entering slide text

Once the Pick a Look Wizard finishes, PowerPoint creates the **title slide**, the first slide in your presentation. The title slide has two **placeholders**, boxes with dashed line borders where you enter text. The title slide has a **title placeholder** labeled "Click to add title" and **a main text placeholder** labeled "Click to add sub-title" where you enter additional information, such as your company name or department. To enter text in a placeholder, simply click the placeholder and then type your text. After you enter text in a placeholder, the placeholder becomes a **text object**. Objects are the building blocks that make up a presentation slide. ▶ Lynn begins working on the president's presentation by entering the title of the presentation in the title placeholder.

1. **Move the pointer over the title placeholder labeled "Click to add title"**
   The pointer changes to I when you move the pointer over the placeholder. The pointer changes shape depending on the task you are trying to accomplish; Table 2-1 describes the functions of the most common PowerPoint mouse pointer shapes.
2. **Click the title placeholder**
   The blinking vertical line, called the **insertion point**, indicates where your text will appear in the title placeholder. A slanted line border, called a **selection box**, appears around the title placeholder, indicating that it is selected and ready to accept text, as shown in Figure 2-6. Lynn enters the title for the presentation.
3. **Type Annual Report, press [Enter], then type Executive Summary**
   PowerPoint centers the title text within the title placeholder, now called a text object. Pressing [Enter] in a text object moves the insertion point down to begin a new line of text.
4. **Click the main text placeholder**
   In the same way, Lynn enters the president of Nomad's name, job title, and meeting date in the main text placeholder.
5. **Type Bill Davidson, press [Enter], type President, press [Enter], then type June 18, 1995**
   Compare your title slide to Figure 2-7.
6. **Click the Selection Tool button on the Drawing toolbar, or click outside the main text object in a blank area of the slide**
   Clicking the Selection Tool button or a blank area of the slide deselects all selected objects on the slide.

TABLE 2-1:
PowerPoint mouse pointer shapes

SHAPE	DESCRIPTION
↖	Appears when you select the Selection tool. Use this pointer to select one or more PowerPoint objects.
I	Appears when you move the pointer over a text object. Use this pointer, referred to as the I-beam, to place the insertion point where you want to begin typing or select text.
✥	Appears when you move the pointer over a bullet or slide icon. Use this pointer to select title or paragraph text.
↓	Appears when you select the Text tool. Use this pointer, referred to as the text cursor, to create text objects.
+	Appears when you select a drawing tool. Use this pointer, referred to as the crosshair cursor, to draw shapes.

FIGURE 2-6: Selected title placeholder

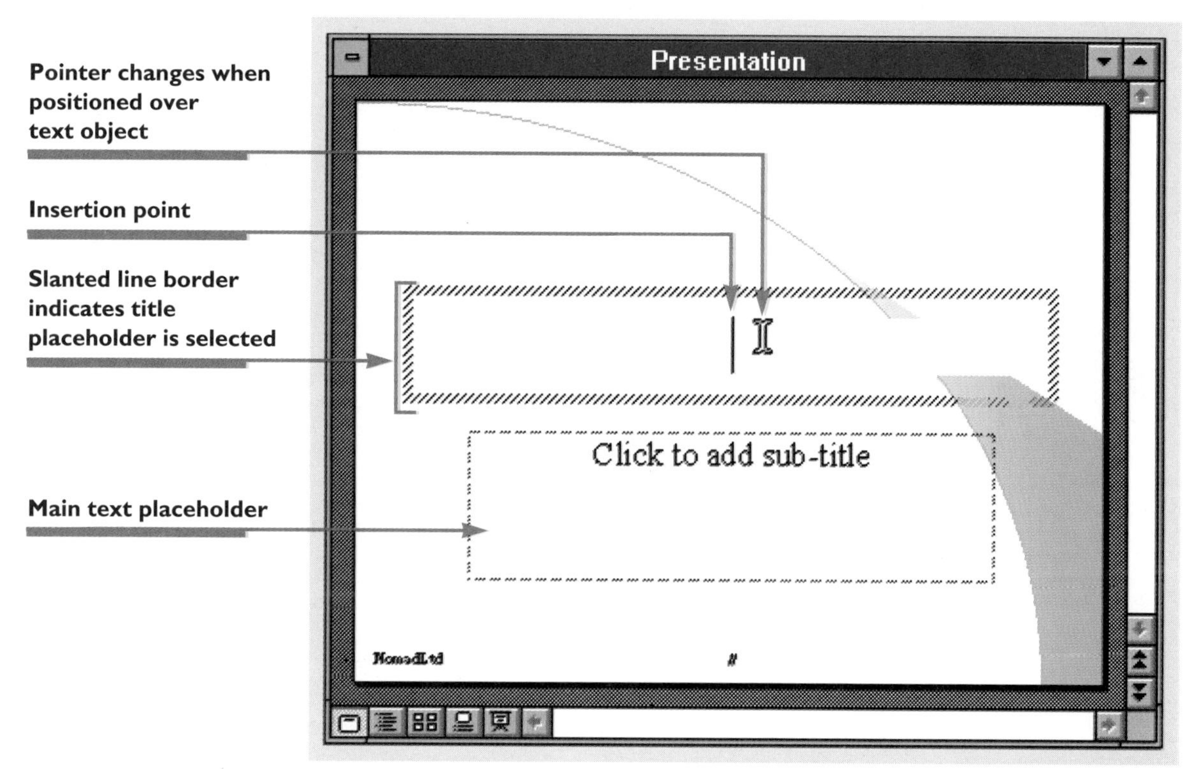

FIGURE 2-7: Title slide with text

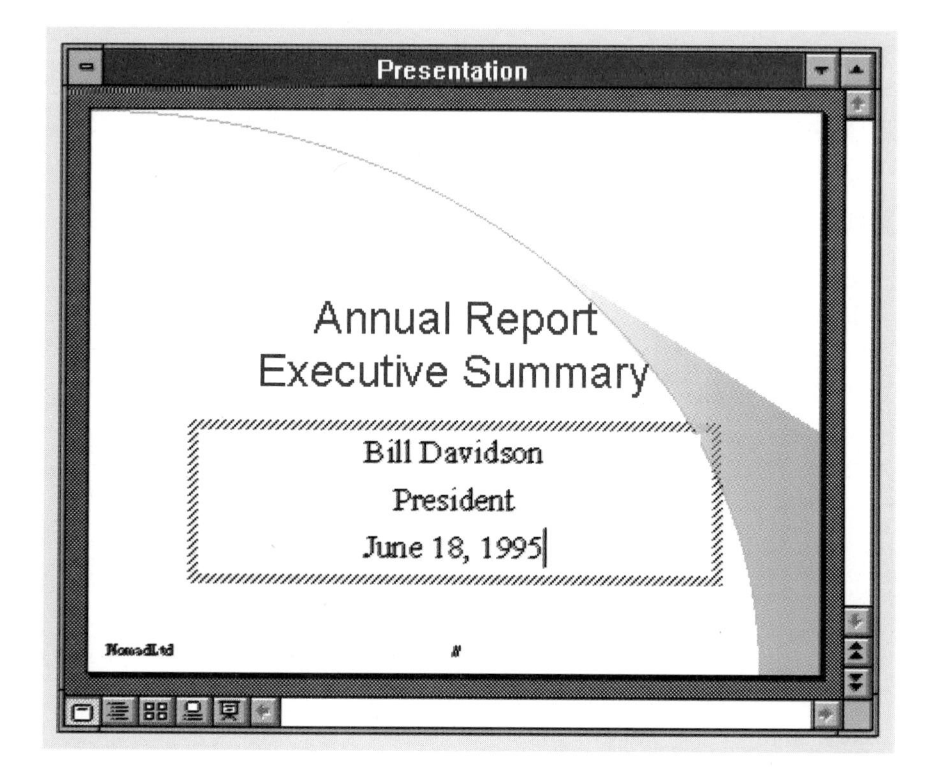

TROUBLE?

If you press a wrong key by mistake, press [Backspace] to erase the character, then continue to type.

Creating a new slide

To help you create a new slide easily, PowerPoint offers 21 predesigned slide layouts, called **AutoLayouts**, that include a variety of placeholder arrangements for titles, main text, and objects such as clip art, graphs, and charts. See Table 2-2 for an explanation of the different placeholders you'll find in the list of AutoLayouts. ▶ To continue developing the presentation, Lynn needs to create a slide that displays the topic headings for the president's presentation.

1. **Click the New Slide button** New Slide... **on the status bar, or click the Insert New Slide button on the Standard toolbar**
   The New Slide dialog box opens, displaying the different AutoLayouts (click the down scroll arrow to see more). You can choose the layout that best meets your needs by clicking it in the AutoLayout list. The title for the selected AutoLayout appears in a Preview box to the right of the list, as shown in Figure 2-8. Lynn decides to use the default Bulleted List AutoLayout to enter the topic headings.
2. **Click OK**
   A new empty slide appears after the current slide in your presentation and displays a title placeholder and a main text placeholder. Notice that the status bar displays Slide 2. Lynn enters a title for this slide.
3. **Click the title placeholder then type Summary**
4. **Click the main text placeholder**
   This deselects the title text object. The insertion point appears next to the bullet in the main text placeholder. Lynn enters the first two topic headings for the president's presentation.
5. **Type Goals, press [Enter], then type Accomplishments**
   A new bullet automatically appears when you press [Enter].
6. **Click the Selection Tool button on the Drawing toolbar, or click outside the main text object in a blank area of the slide to deselect the main text object**
   Compare your slide to Figure 2-9.

TABLE 2-2: AutoLayout placeholder types

PLACEHOLDER	DESCRIPTION
Bulleted List	Displays a short list of related points
Clip Art	Inserts a picture, such as PowerPoint clip art
Graph	Inserts a graph that uses standard Microsoft graph techniques
Org Chart	Inserts an organizational chart
Table	Inserts a table from Microsoft Word
Object	Adds an external object such as a media clip, sound, or WordArt to a PowerPoint slide

FIGURE 2-8: New Slide dialog box

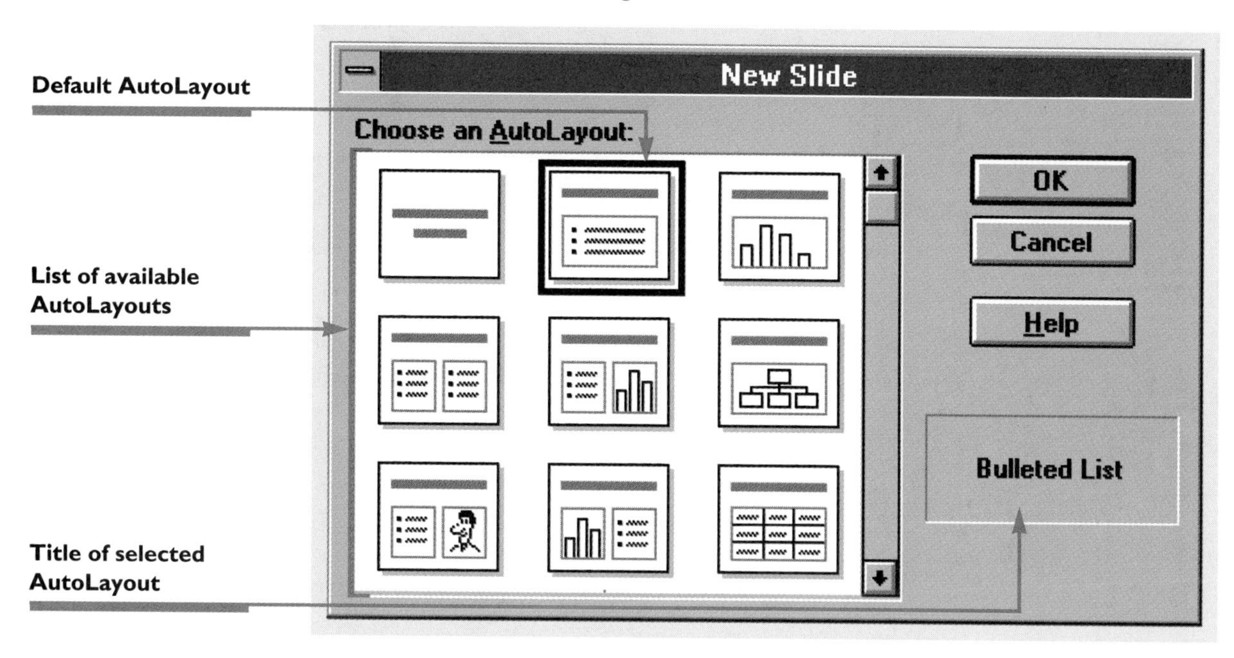

FIGURE 2-9: New slide with bulleted list

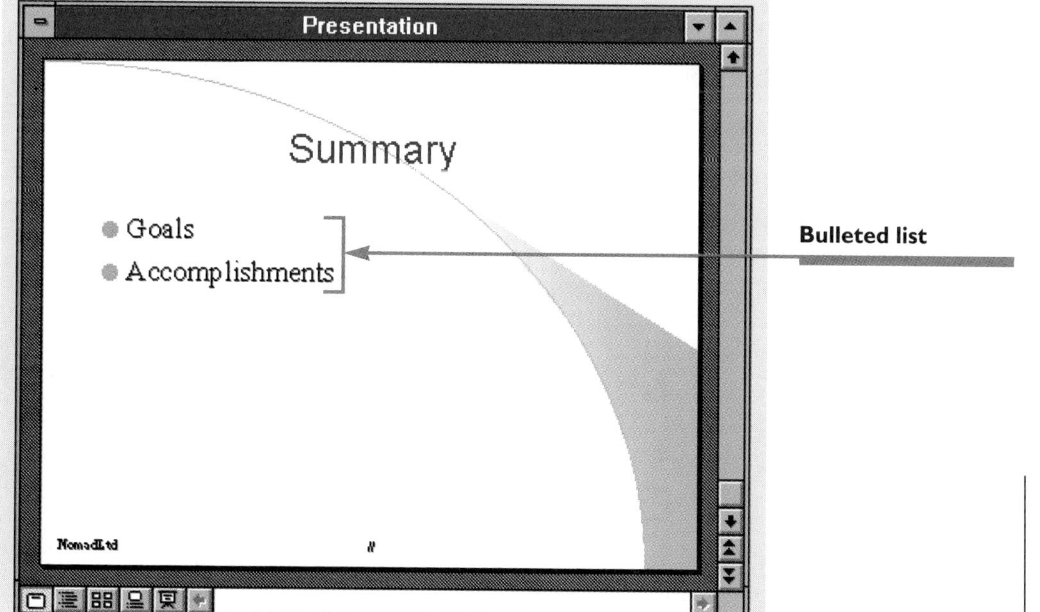

QUICK TIP

You can move from one text object to the next using the shortcut key [Ctrl][Enter]. ▶ To add a new slide with the same layout as the current slide, press and hold [Shift] then click the New Slide button New Slide... on the status bar.■

Working in Outline view

In PowerPoint, you can enter your presentation text in Slide view or Outline view. Outline view displays the titles and main text of all the slides in your presentation in one view. As in a regular outline, the headings, or **titles**, appear first, then under them, the sub points, or **main text**. The main text appears as one or more lines of bulleted text under a title. ▶ Lynn entered the first two slides of her presentation in Slide view. Now, she switches to Outline view to enter text for two more slides.

1 **Click the Outline View button on the status bar**
The outline fills the Presentation window with the Slide 2 title selected (the one you just created). Notice that the Outlining toolbar replaces the Drawing toolbar on the left side of the PowerPoint window. Table 2-3 describes the buttons available on the Outlining toolbar. Now, Lynn enters the text for her third slide.

2 Click the **Insert New Slide button** on the Standard toolbar, then type **Goals**
A symbol called a **slide icon** appears when you add a new slide to the outline. Text you enter next to a slide icon becomes the title for that slide. Now Lynn enters the main text for the Goals slide.

3 Press **[Enter]** then click the **Demote (Indent More) button** on the Outlining toolbar, or press **[Tab]**
The slide icon changes to a bullet and indents one level to the right.

4 Type **Increase overall product sales by 35%**, then press **[Enter]**; type **Increase travel expeditions by 30%**, then press **[Enter]**; type **Increase environmental funding by 50%**, then press **[Ctrl] [Enter]**
Notice that pressing [Ctrl] [Enter] creates a new slide.

5 Type **Accomplishments** then press **[Ctrl] [Enter]**; type **Product sales up by 53.4%**, then press **[Enter]**; type **Environmental funding up by 5.4%** then press **[Enter]**; type **Travel expeditions up by 26.9%**
Lynn discovers that two of the bullet points she just typed for slide four are out of order so she moves them into the correct position.

6 Position the pointer over the last bullet in Slide 4, then click
The pointer changes from I to ✣, and PowerPoint selects the entire line of text.

7 Click the **Move Up button** on the Outlining toolbar
The third bullet point moves up one line and trades places with the second bullet point, as shown in Figure 2-10. Now, Lynn wants to see the slides she just created in Slide view.

8 Double-click the **slide icon** for Slide 4, then view the slide
PowerPoint switches to Slide view for Slide 4.

9 Click the **Previous Slide button** below the vertical scroll bar three times to view each slide until Slide 1 appears in the status bar

FIGURE 2-10: Outline view

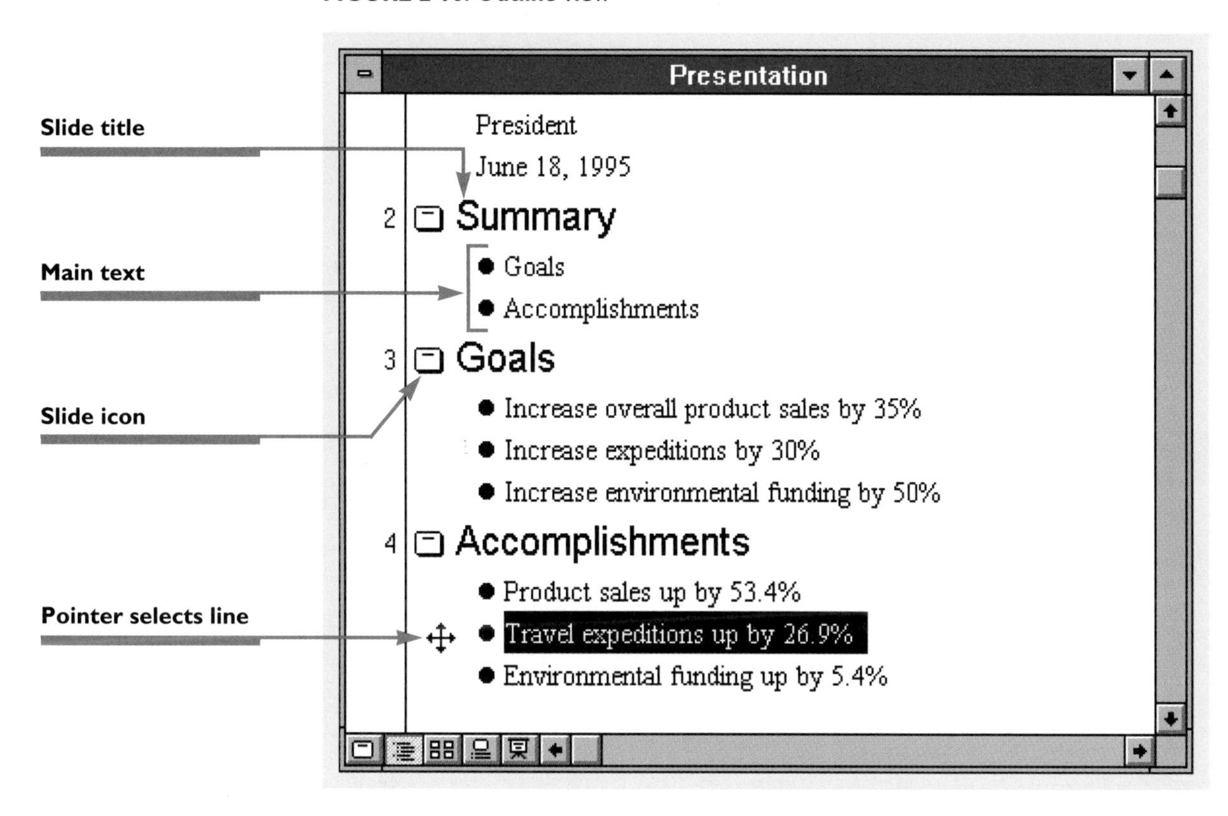

TABLE 2-3:
Outlining toolbar commands

BUTTON	DESCRIPTION
Promote (Indent less)	Indents selected text one tab to the left
Demote (Indent more)	Indents selected text one tab to the right
Move Up	Moves the selection above the previous line
Move Down	Moves the selection below the next line
Collapse Selection	Displays only the titles of the selection
Expand Selection	Displays all levels of the selection
Show Titles	Displays only the titles for all slides
Show All	Displays the title and all the body text for all slides
Show Formatting	Displays all character formatting

QUICK **TIP**

You can use the mouse to move titles and main text by dragging slide icons or bullets to a new location.■

Entering text in Notes Pages view

To help you give your presentation, you can create speaker's notes that accompany your slides so you don't have to rely on your memory. Notes Pages view displays a reduced slide image and a text placeholder where you enter the notes for each slide of your presentation. The notes you enter there do not appear on the slides themselves; they are private notes for you. You can also print these pages. See the Quick Tip and the related topic "Printing handout pages" for more information. ▶ To make sure the president doesn't forget key points of his presentation, Lynn enters notes for some of the slides.

1. Click the **Notes Pages View button** on the status bar
   The view of your presentation changes from Slide view to Notes Pages view, as shown in Figure 2-11.
2. Click the **text placeholder** below the slide image
   The insertion point appears, indicating the placeholder is ready to accept your text. The insertion point is small and difficult to see so Lynn increases the view size.
3. Click the **Zoom Control button** on the Standard toolbar, then click **66%**
   The text placeholder increases in size. Now that the text placeholder is larger and easier to see, Lynn enters her notes for Slide 1.
4. Type **Welcome to the 1994 Annual Report meeting for shareholders and employees**
5. Click the **Next Slide button** below the vertical scroll bar, click the **text placeholder**, then type **The main purpose for this meeting is to share with you the exciting accomplishments Nomad Ltd has achieved in the last year**
   As you type, text automatically wraps to the next line.
6. Click , click the **text placeholder**, then type **Our 1994 goals were aggressive yet attainable. We started 1994 with the desire to increase product sales by 35%, increase travel expeditions by 30%, and increase funding on the environment by 50%. Well, how did we do?**
7. Click , click the **text placeholder**, type **With the introduction of our award winning OutBack camping gear series, product sales jumped up by 53.4%. With the acquisition of a travel subsidiary company called New Directions, expeditions for the year increased by 26.9%. Because of new product lines and the acquisition of New Directions, environmental funding only increased by 5.4%.**; press **[Enter]**, then type **I would like to thank you all for your hard work. Congratulations!**
8. Click the **Zoom Control button** then click **33%**
   The view size decreases to 33%, as shown in Figure 2-12. Now Lynn can save her work.

FIGURE 2-11: Notes Pages view

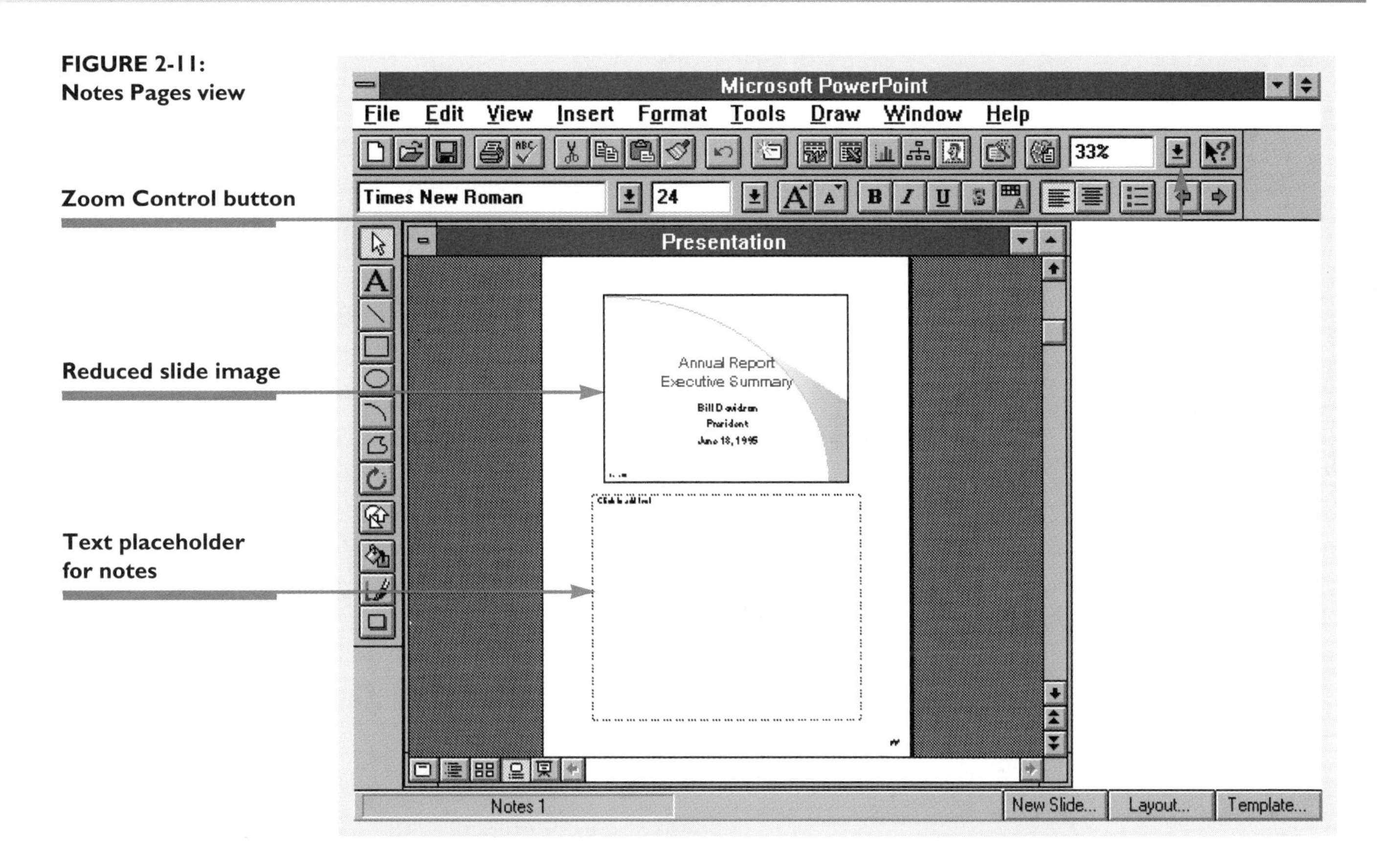

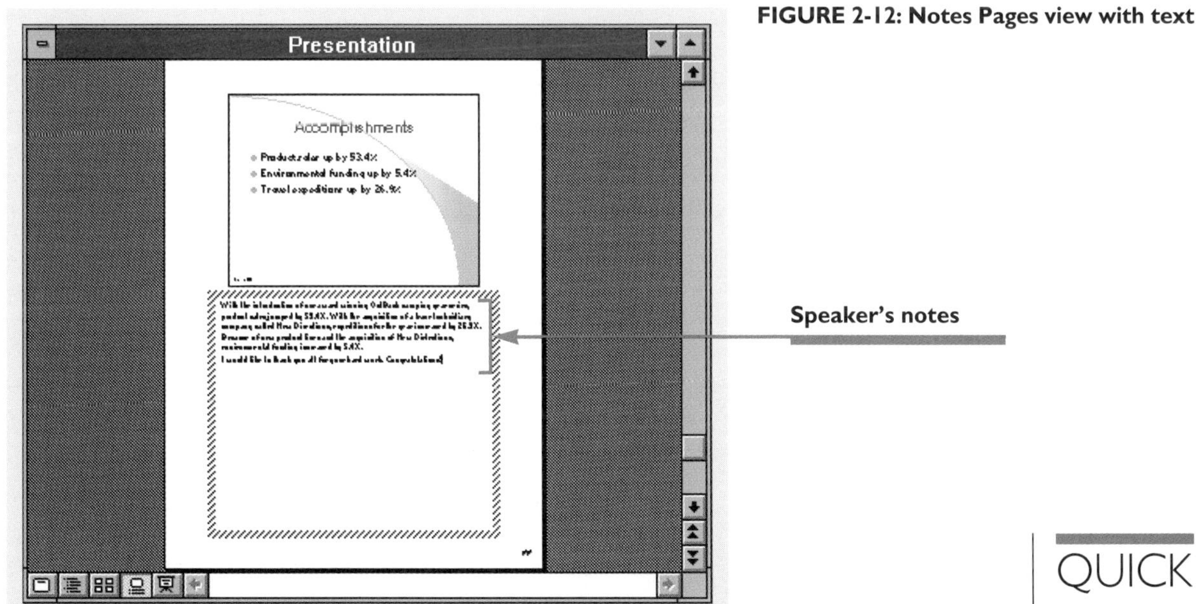

FIGURE 2-12: Notes Pages view with text

Printing handout pages

You can also print pages for your audience so they can follow along as you make your presentation. You can print handout pages that contain either two, three, or six slide pictures per page. In the Print dialog box, select the desired handout pages setting, and then print.

QUICK TIP

If you want to provide pages on which your audience can take notes, print the Notes Pages view, but leave the text placeholder blank or draw some lines.■

Saving a presentation

To store a presentation permanently, you must save it to a file on a disk. As a general rule, you should save your work about every 10 or 15 minutes and before printing. ▶ Name and save the president's presentation to the MY_FILES directory you created on your Student Disk. For more information about your Student Disk, refer to "Read This Before You Begin Microsoft PowerPoint 4.0" on page 2 of PowerPoint Unit 1. Lynn saves her presentation as 94REPORT.

1. **Click File on the menu bar, then click Save As**
   The Save As dialog box opens.
2. **If necessary, double-click the File Name text box to select its contents**
   You edit the text in the File Name text box the same way you would edit text in an outline. PowerPoint accepts filenames consisting of one to eight characters.
3. **Type 94REPORT in the File Name text box**
   The name "94REPORT" appears in the File Name text box, replacing the PowerPoint default filename.
4. **Click the Drives list arrow, then click the drive that contains your Student Disk**
   See Figure 2-13. Windows displays an error message if you select a drive that does not contain a disk. See the related topic "Select the correct drive when saving a file" for more information.

   If you created a MY_FILES directory in "Microsoft Windows 3.1," you can save your files there. If you do not have a MY_FILES directory, skip Step 5 and continue with Step 6 to save the file to the a:\ directory on your Student Disk.
5. **Double-click the MY_FILES directory on your Student Disk**
   The Save As dialog displays the location on your Student Disk where you will save your presentation.
6. **Click OK**
   The Summary Info dialog box opens, displaying title, subject, and author information about your presentation. Closing this dialog box saves the presentation with the filename 94REPORT.PPT. The default file extension for PowerPoint presentations is PPT.
7. **Click the Subject text box, type 1994 Annual Report, then click OK**
   The Summary dialog box closes, and the filename appears in the title bar at the top of the Presentation window. Lynn decides she wants to save the presentation in Slide view instead of Notes Pages view so it opens to display a slide.
8. **Click the Slide View button on the status bar**
   The presentation view changes from Notes Pages view to Slide view.
9. **Click the Save button on the Standard toolbar**
   The Save command saves your changes to the file you designated when you used Save As. Save a file frequently while working with it to protect the presentation. Table 2-4 shows the difference between the Save and the Save As commands.

FIGURE 2-13: Save As dialog box

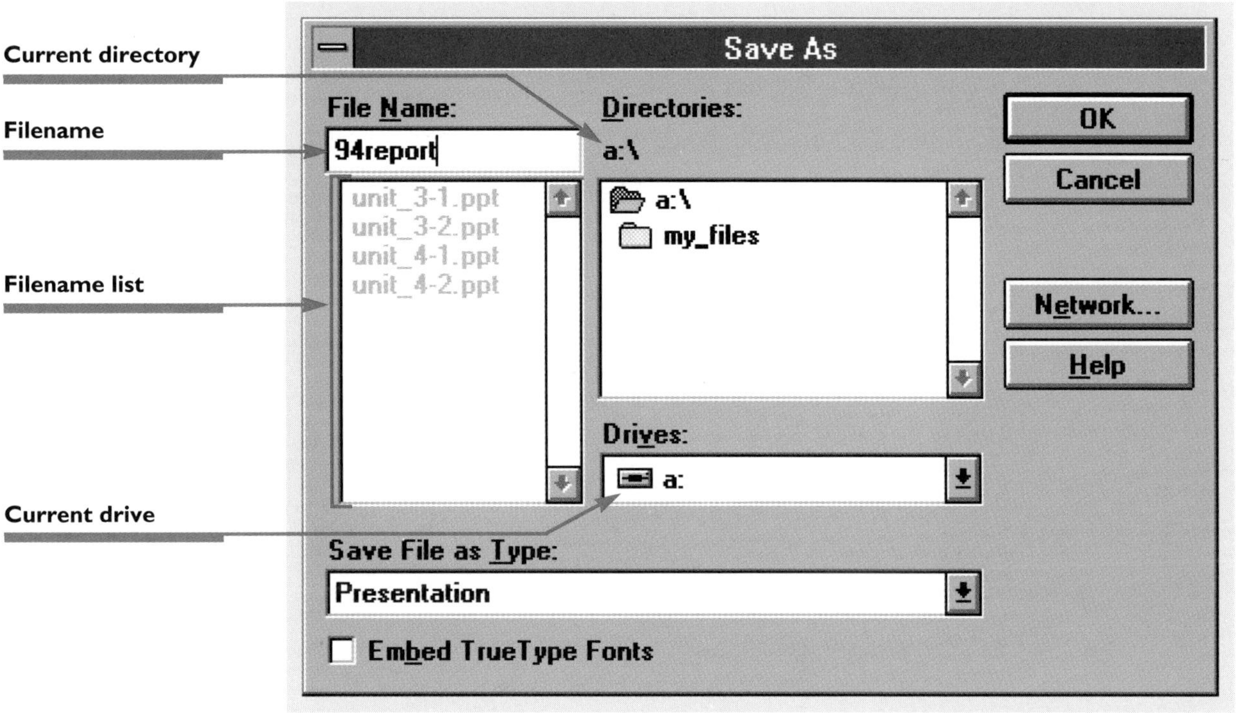

Current directory

Filename

Filename list

Current drive

Selecting the correct drive when saving a file

When you save a file, you need to select the appropriate disk drive on the computer—either drive A or drive B. You generally do not save files on the internal hard disk, drive C, or network server drive (D, E, and so on) unless you are working on your own computer. Instead, save all your work on a 3.5- or 5.25-inch disk. To create a backup copy, save the file on a second disk and store the second disk in a safe place.

QUICK TIP

Click the Save button on the Standard toolbar to save a file quickly, or use the shortcut key [Ctrl][S].

TABLE 2-4: Save and Save As commands

COMMAND	DESCRIPTION	PURPOSE
Save As	Gives you opportunity to designate a location and name for file	Use to save a file for the first time, change the file's name or location, or save the file to use in a different application. Useful to save different versions of a presentation.
Save	Saves named file to previously specified location	Use to save any changes to the original file. Fast and easy; do this often to protect your work.

Printing a presentation

Print your presentation when you have completed it or when you want to review your work. Reviewing hard copies of your presentation at different stages of production is helpful and gives you an overall perspective of your presentation content and look. Table 2-5 provides some printing guidelines. ▶ Lynn prints the slides and notes pages of the presentation to review what she has developed so far.

1. Check the printer
   Make sure the printer is on, has paper, and that it is on-line or ready to print. If you send a file to a printer that is not ready, an error message appears.
2. Click **File** on the menu bar, then click **Print**
   The Print dialog box opens, as shown in Figure 2-14. In this dialog box, you can specify the print options you want to use when you print your presentation. With the Print What option set to Slides and the Slide Range option set to All, Lynn is ready to print all the slides of the presentation.
3. Click **OK**
   PowerPoint sends the file to the printer. Note that the Cancel button displays on the screen briefly, giving you a chance to cancel the print job.
4. Click **File** on the menu bar, then click **Print**
   The Print dialog box again opens. You have already printed the presentation slides. Now print the notes pages.
5. Click the **Print What list arrow**, then click **Notes Pages**
   PowerPoint is ready to print the Notes Pages view of the presentation.
6. Click **OK**
   The Print dialog box closes, and your presentation is printed.
7. Click **File** on the menu bar, then click **Exit**
   The presentation file closes and you exit PowerPoint.

TABLE 2-5:
Presentation printing guidelines

BEFORE YOU PRINT	RECOMMENDATION
Check the printer	Make sure the printer is on and on-line, that it has paper, and there are no error messages or warning signals.
Check the Slide Setup	Make sure the slide size, orientation, and page number are acceptable for the printer by choosing the Slide Setup command from the File menu.
Check the printer selection	Check the printer entry at the top of the Print dialog box. If the incorrect printer is selected, click the Printer button to select the correct printer.

FIGURE 2-14: Print dialog box

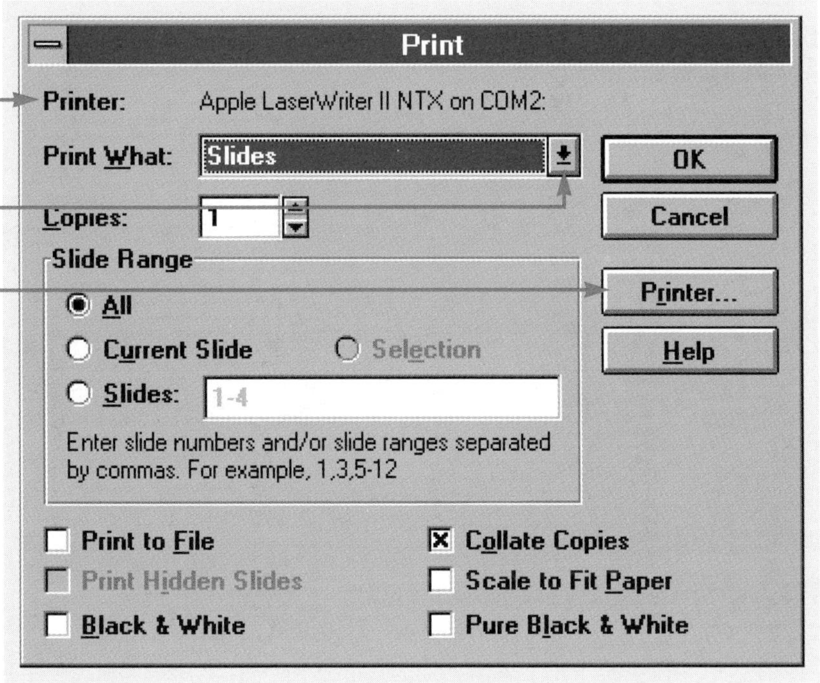

Current printer

Click to display list of available options to print

Click to specify new printer

Print

Printer: Apple LaserWriter II NTX on COM2:

Print What: Slides

Copies: 1

OK

Cancel

Printer...

Help

Slide Range

All

Current Slide

Selection

Slides: 1-4

Enter slide numbers and/or slide ranges separated by commas. For example, 1,3,5-12

Print to File

Print Hidden Slides

Black & White

Collate Copies

Scale to Fit Paper

Pure Black & White

Using Slide Setup

Use the Slide Setup command on the File menu to customize the presentation output size to meet your specific needs. You can change the slide width, height, and orientation of your slides.

QUICK TIP

Click the Print button on the Standard toolbar to print quickly using the current settings.

CONCEPTS REVIEW

Label each of the elements of the PowerPoint window shown in Figure 2-15.

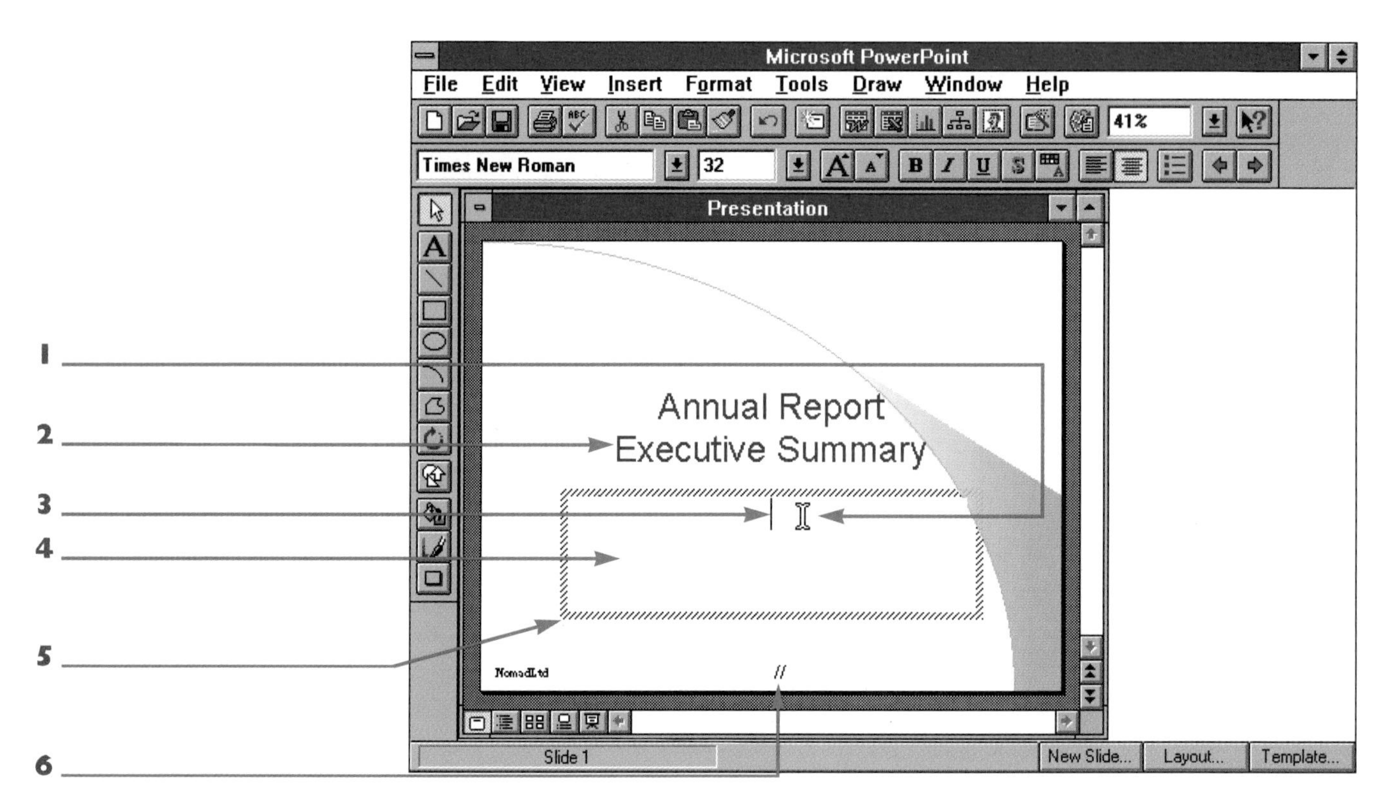

FIGURE 2-15

Match each of the terms with the statement that describes its function.

7 A symbol that initially appears after clicking the main text placeholder

8 A symbol that indicates where your text will appear in a text object

9 A slanted line selection box with text

10 A dotted box with prompt text that displays on a slide where you can enter text

11 A symbol that represents a slide

a. Placeholder
b. Insertion point
c. Text object
d. Slide icon
e. Bullet

Select the best answer from the list of choices.

12 Which of the following is NOT a presentation print option?

a. Slides
b. Notes Pages
c. Handouts (4 slides per page)
d. Outline view

13 Which of the following is NOT a slide output option?

a. 35-mm slides
b. B&W overheads
c. Notes pages
d. On-screen slide show

14 When you start a new presentation, which command do you choose from the PowerPoint startup dialog box to choose a look for your presentation?

a. AutoContent Wizard

b. Pick a Look Wizard

c. Blank Presentation

d. Current Presentation

15 You can make copy of a presentation with a different name by using which command:

a. Save

b. Open

c. Save As

d. Copy

APPLICATIONS REVIEW

1 Choose a look for your presentation.

a. Start PowerPoint.

b. Click the Blank Presentation radio button or click the New button on the Standard toolbar.

c. Click the Pick a Look Wizard radio button, click OK, then click Next.

d. Click the 35mm Slides button, click Next, click each of the template options to review the different designs or use the More button, choose a slide design, then click Apply or Next if using one of the radio button templates.

e. Click Next, click the Audience Handout Pages check box and click the Outline Pages check box to deselect these options, then click Next to continue.

f. Click the Name, company, or other text check box, enter your name in the box, click the Date check box, click the Page Number check box, then click Next.

g. Click the Name, company, or other text check box, click the Date check box, click Next, then click Finish.

2 Enter slide text.

a. Click the title placeholder then type "Product Marketing."

b. Click the main text placeholder, type "Chris Thielen," press [Enter], then type "Manager."

3 Create a new slide and work in Outline view.

a. Switch to Outline view.

b. Click the New Slide button

c. Enter the outline from Table 2-6.

TABLE 2-6

Goals for the Week
- Chris
  - Interview new candidates
- John
  - Revise product marketing report
  - Set up plan for the annual sales meeting
- April
  - Investigate advertising agencies
  - Establish advertising budget

4 Enter text in Notes Pages view.

a. Switch to Notes Pages view for Slide 2.

b. Click the notes placeholder.

c. Zoom in the view.

d. Enter the following speaker's notes:

Remember, this week I'll be interviewing new candidates for a product marketing position. I'll have each of you interview the candidates who meet initial qualifications next week.

e. Switch back to Slide view.

5 Print a handout (2 slides per page) and the notes pages.

a. Click File on the menu bar, then click Print.

b. Click the Print What list arrow, click Handouts (2 slides per page), then click OK.

c. Using the same process, print the notes pages to accompany the handouts.

d. Save the presentation as INTRVIEW.PPT in the MY_FILES directory on your Student Disk.

6 Create a new presentation.

a. Click the New button on the Standard toolbar.

b. Click the Blank Presentation radio button in the PowerPoint startup dialog box.

c. Click the Bulleted List AutoLayout, then click OK.

d. Enter the slide title and bulleted text in Table 2-7.

TABLE 2-7

Title:	Next Steps
Bulleted Text:	Develop Technology Implementation Plans
	Develop Marketing Implementation Plans

e. Print the slides and the notes pages to accompany the presentation.

f. Save the presentation as NEXTSTEP.PPT in the MY_FILES directory on your Student Disk, and close the presentation.

INDEPENDENT CHALLENGE 1

You have been asked to give a six-week basic computer course at the local adult school for adults who have never used a computer. One of your responsibilities as the instructor is to create presentation slides and an outline of the course materials for the students.

Plan and create presentation slides that outline the course material for the students. Create slides for the course introduction, course description, course requirements, course texts and grading, and a detailed course syllabus. For each slide include speaker's notes to help you stay on track during the presentation.

Create your own course material, but assume the following: the school has a computer lab with IBM compatible and Microsoft Windows software; each student has a computer on his or her desk; students are intimidated by computers but want to learn; each weekly class session lasts for 50 minutes.

To complete this independent challenge:

1. Think about the results you want to see, the information you need, and the type of message you want to communicate in this presentation.
2. Sketch a sample presentation on a piece of paper, indicating the presentation look and how the information should be laid out. What content should go on the slides? On the notes pages?
3. Create the presentation by choosing a presentation look, entering the title slide text, the outline text, and the notes pages text. Remember you are creating and entering your own presentation material.
4. Save the presentation as CLASS1.PPT in the MY_FILES directory on your Student Disk. Before printing, view each slide so you know what the presentation will look like. Adjust any items as needed, and print the slides, notes pages, and handouts.
5. Submit your presentation plan, your preliminary sketches, and the final worksheet printout.

INDEPENDENT CHALLENGE 2

You are the training director for Space Amusements, Inc., a theme park and entertainment company. One of your responsibilities is to give an introductory presentation at the weekly new employee orientation training class. The theme park, Space Amusements, is hiring 30 to 50 new employees a week for the peak season in the areas of entertainment, customer support, maintenance, cashier, and food service.

Plan and create presentation slides that outline your part of the training for new employees. Create slides for the introduction, agenda, company history, new attractions, benefits, and safety requirements. For each slide include speaker's notes that you can hand out to the employees.

Create your own presentation and company material, but assume the following: the new employee training class lasts for four hours; the training director's presentation lasts 15 minutes; the new attraction for this season is the Demon roller coaster.

To complete this independent challenge:

1. Think about the results you want to see, the information you need, and what type of message you want to communicate for this presentation.
2. Sketch a sample presentation on a piece of paper, indicating the presentation look and how the information should be laid out. What content should go on the slides? On the notes pages?
3. Create the presentation by choosing a presentation look, entering the title slide text, the outline text, and the notes pages text. Remember you are creating and entering your own presentation material.
4. Save the presentation as NEWHIRE.PPT in the MY_FILES directory on your Student Disk. Before printing, view each slide so you know what the presentation will look like. Adjust any items as needed, and print the slides and notes pages.
5. Submit your presentation plan, your preliminary sketches, and the final worksheet printout.

UNIT 3

OBJECTIVES

- ▶ Open an existing presentation
- ▶ Add and arrange text
- ▶ Format text
- ▶ Draw and modify objects
- ▶ Edit objects
- ▶ Align and group objects
- ▶ Replace text
- ▶ Check spelling

A PRESENTATION

fter you create the basic outline of your presentation and enter text, you need to review your work and modify your slides to achieve the best possible look. In this unit, you will open an existing presentation, and then add and rearrange text, draw and modify objects, replace a font, and use the spell checker. ▶ Lynn Shaw continues to work on the Annual Report Executive Summary presentation for the president of Nomad Ltd. Lynn uses PowerPoint's text editing and drawing features to refine the presentation and bring it closer to a finished look. ▶

Opening an existing presentation

Sometimes it's easiest to create a new presentation by changing an existing one. Creating a new presentation from an old one saves you from having to type duplicate information. You simply open the file you want to change, then use the Save As command to save a copy of the file with a new name. In this book, whenever you open an existing presentation, the instructions tell you to save a copy of it to your Student Disk so you can keep the original file intact. Saving a copy with a new name does not affect the information in the original file. Table 3-1 lists some guidelines to follow when naming a presentation file. ▶ Follow Lynn as she opens an existing presentation and saves it using a new name.

1 Start PowerPoint and insert your Student Disk in the appropriate disk drive

2 Click the **Open an Existing Presentation radio button** in the PowerPoint startup dialog box, then click **OK**
If PowerPoint is already running, click the Open button on the Standard toolbar to open this dialog box.

The Open dialog box opens.

3 Click the **Drives list arrow**
A list of drives opens. Locate the drive that contains your Student Disk. These lessons assume your Student Disk is in drive A.

4 Click **a:**
A list of the files on your Student Disk appears in the File Name list box, as shown in Figure 3-1.

5 In the File Name list box, click **UNIT_3-1.PPT** then click **OK**
The file named UNIT_3-1.PPT opens. Now, save a copy of this file with a new name to the MY_FILES directory on your Student Disk using the Save As command.

For more information on the MY_FILES directory, see the lesson entitled "Saving a presentation" in Unit 1.

6 Click **File** on the menu bar, then click **Save As**
The Save As dialog box opens. The Save As dialog box works just like the Open dialog box.

7 Make sure the Drives list box displays the drive containing your Student Disk, then double-click **MY_FILES** in the list of directories
If you aren't saving files to the MY_FILES directory, you don't need to double-click it. Continue with Step 8.

8 If necessary, select the current filename in the File Name text box, then type **94REPRT1**
Compare your screen to the Save As dialog box in Figure 3-2.

9 Click **OK**; if the Summary Info dialog box opens, click **OK** again
PowerPoint creates a copy of UNIT_3-1.PPT with the name 94REPRT1.PPT and closes UNIT_3-1.PPT.

FIGURE 3-1: Open dialog box

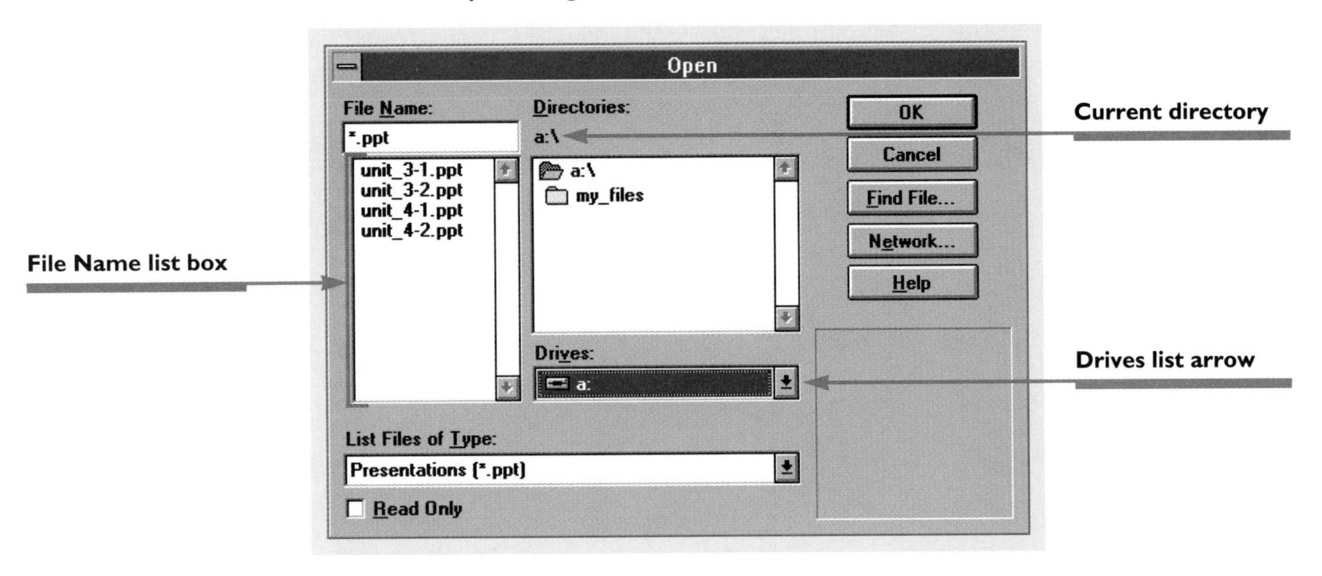

FIGURE 3-2: Save As dialog box

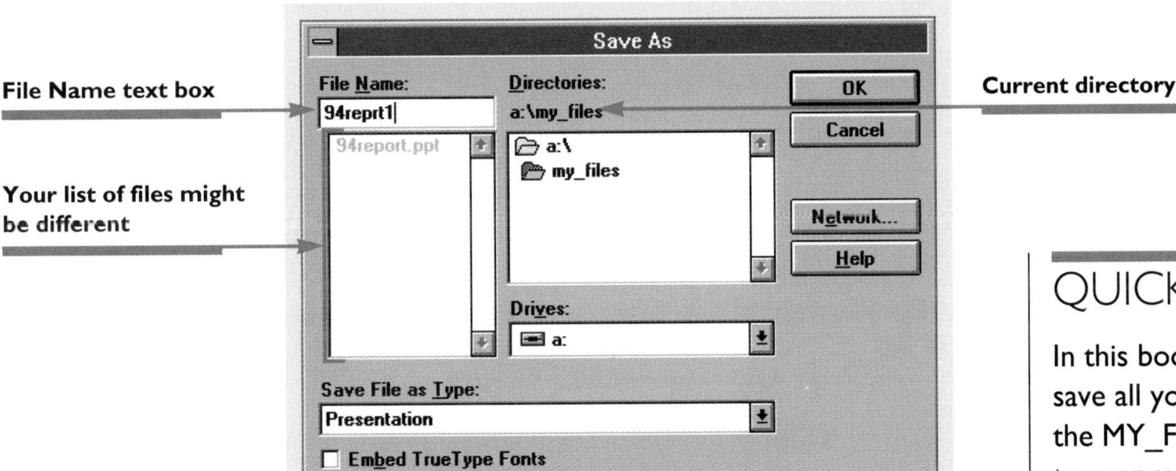

QUICK TIP

In this book, you will save all your work to the MY_FILES directory on your Student Disk that you created in "Microsoft Windows 3.1." This will help you to distinguish between the files that were provided on the Student Disk and the files you modify and save. If you did not create a MY_FILES directory, save all your work to your Student Disk in drive A or drive B.■

TABLE 3-1: Filenaming guidelines

• You can use up to eight characters to name a file.
• Filenames can use uppercase, lowercase, or mixed case.
• You can't use certain special characters, such as /, \, [,], ", and =.
• Filenames can't contain spaces.

Adding and arranging text

Using PowerPoint's advanced text editing capabilities, you can easily add, insert, or rearrange text. On a PowerPoint slide, you either enter text in prearranged text placeholders or use the Text tool to create your own text objects when the text placeholders don't provide the flexibility you need. With the Text tool, you can create two types of text objects: a **text label** used for a small phrase where text doesn't automatically wrap inside a box, and a **word processing box** used for a sentence or paragraph where the text wraps inside the boundaries of a box. ▶ In this lesson, Lynn scrolls to Slide 3 and uses the Text tool to create a word processing box to enter Nomad Ltd's mission statement.

1. Drag the elevator down the vertical scroll bar until the Slide Indicator box displays Slide 3, then release the mouse button
   The Slide Indicator box that appears when you drag the elevator tells you which slide will appear when you release the mouse button. Now, Lynn creates a word processing box and enters the company mission statement next to the shuttle graphic.
2. Click the **Text Tool button** [A] on the Drawing toolbar, then position the pointer in the blank area of the slide
   The pointer changes to ↓.
3. Position the pointer about ½" from the left edge of the slide and about even with the top of the shuttle graphic already on the slide
4. Drag the word processing box toward the graphic so that your screen looks like Figure 3-3
   When you begin dragging, the pointer changes from ↓ to + and an outline of the box appears, indicating how large a text object you are drawing. After you release the mouse, an insertion point appears inside the text object, ready to accept text.
5. Type **Nomad Ltd is a national sporting-goods retailer dedicated to delivering high-quality sporting gear and adventure clothing**
   Notice that the word processing box increases in size as your text wraps inside the object. Lynn discovers a mistake in the mission statement and corrects it by moving a word to its correct position.
6. Double-click the word **adventure** to select it
   When you select the word, the pointer changes from I to ↖.
7. Drag the word **adventure** to the left of the word "sporting" in the mission statement, then release the mouse button
   Notice that the dotted insertion line indicates where PowerPoint will place the word when you release the mouse button.
8. Click a blank area of the slide outside the text object
   The text object deselects. Your screen to should look similar to Figure to 3-4.

FIGURE 3-3: Slide showing word processing box ready to accept text

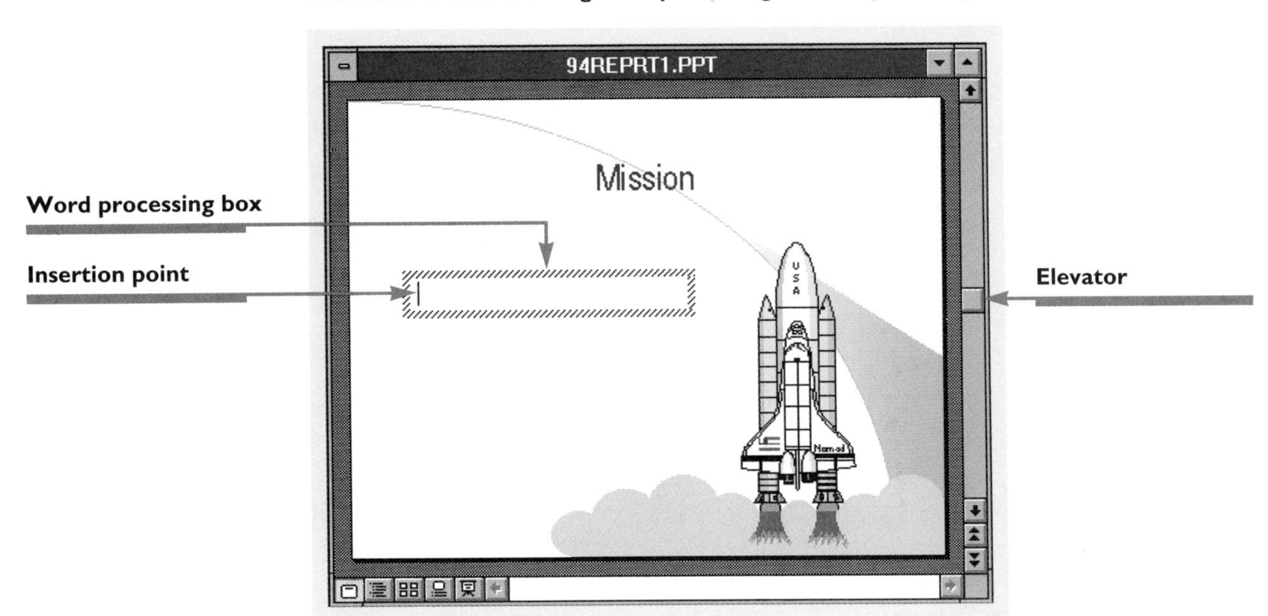

FIGURE 3-4: Slide after adding text to a word processing box

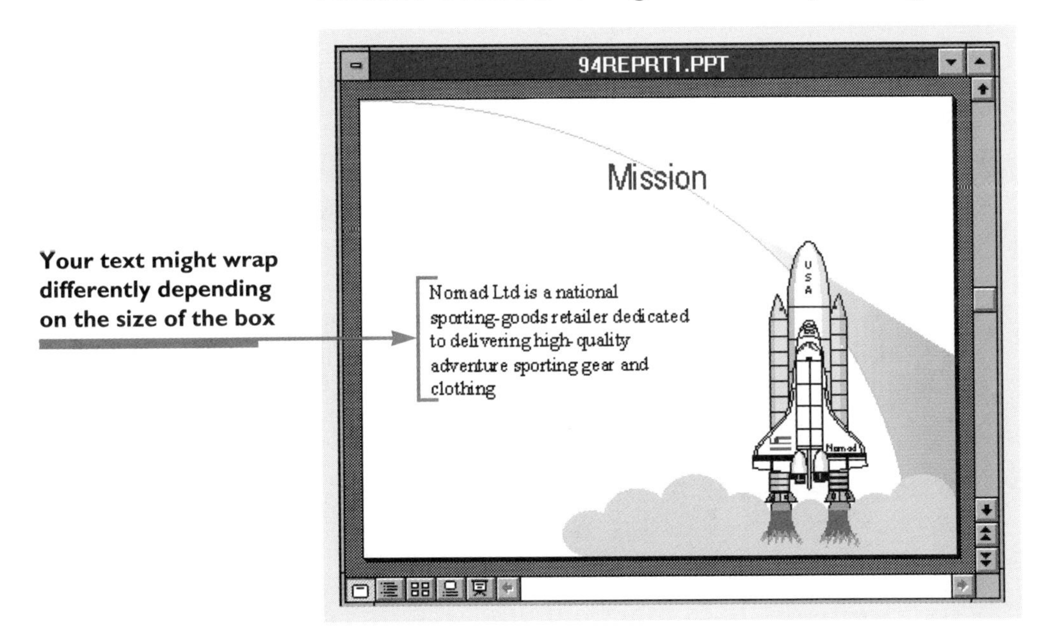

Formatting text

Once you have entered and arranged the text in your presentation, you can change and modify the way the text looks to emphasize the message you are presenting. Text that is important needs to be highlighted in some way to make it distinct from other text or objects on the slide. To change the way text looks, you need to select it, and then choose one of the Formatting commands to make the change. ▶ Lynn uses some of the commands on the Formatting toolbar to change the way the company mission statement looks.

1. **Press [Shift] then click the word processing box**
   A **dotted selection box** appears around the word processing box, which indicates that the whole text object is selected, not just the text inside the object. Lynn selects the text object instead of individual text because she wants to make a **global change**, which changes all of the text. Now, Lynn changes the size and appearance of the text to emphasize it on the slide.
2. Click the **Increase Font Size button** and the **Italic button** on the Formatting toolbar
   The text increases in size and changes from normal to italic text. The Italic button, like the Bold button, is a toggle button, which you click to turn the attribute on or off. Lynn decides to change the mission statement text color.
3. Click the **Text Color button** on the Formatting toolbar
   A color menu appears, displaying the available text colors.
4. Click the **gold color cell**, as shown in Figure 3-5
   The text in the word processing box changes color. Now, Lynn puts the finishing touch on the mission statement by changing the font.
5. Click the **Font button** on the Formatting toolbar
   A list of available fonts opens, as shown in Figure 3-6. The double line at the top of the font list separates the most recent fonts you used from the rest of the available fonts. Lynn finds and chooses the Arial font to replace the current font in the text object.
6. Click the **down scroll arrow** if necessary, then click **Arial**
   The Arial font replaces the original font in the text object. Compare your screen to Figure 3-7.
7. Click a blank area of the slide outside the text object to deselect the text object
8. Click the **Next Slide button** to move to Slide 4, which you'll work with in the next lesson

FIGURE 3-5:
Text Color menu

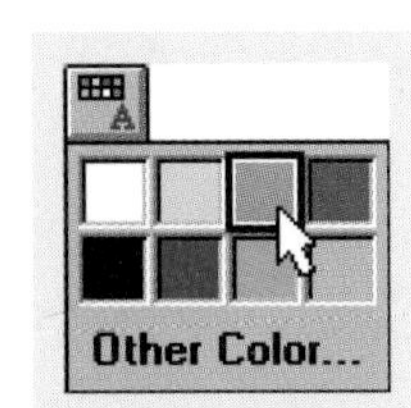

FIGURE 3-6:
Font list

Your list of fonts might be different

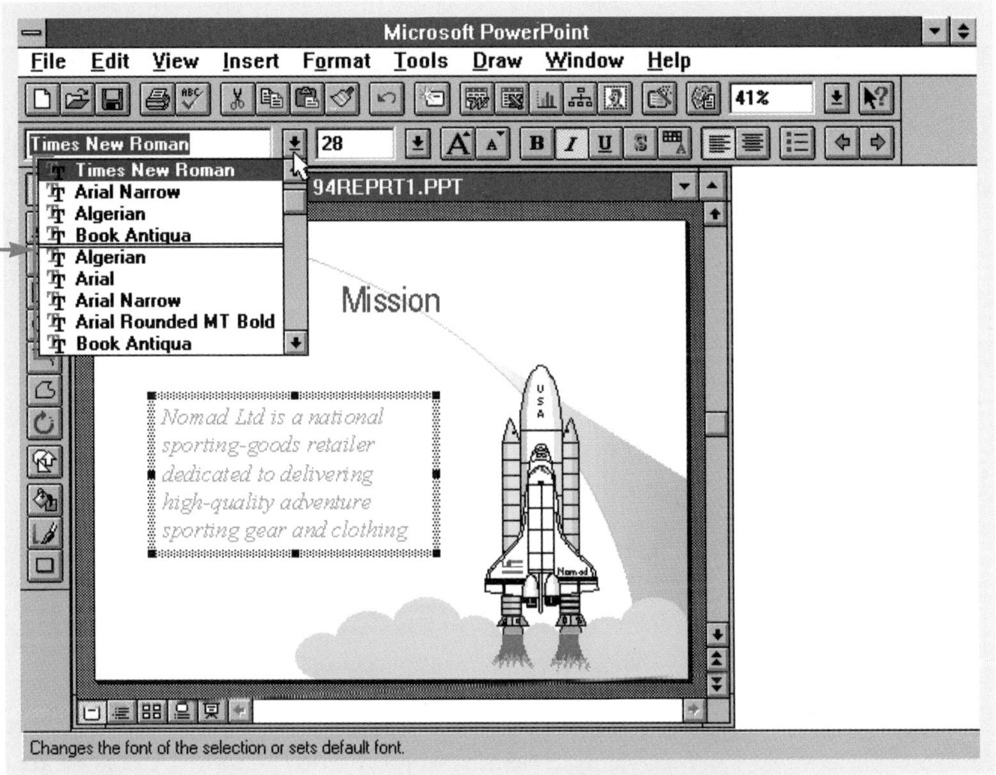

FIGURE 3-7:
Slide showing formatted word processing box

Dotted selection box

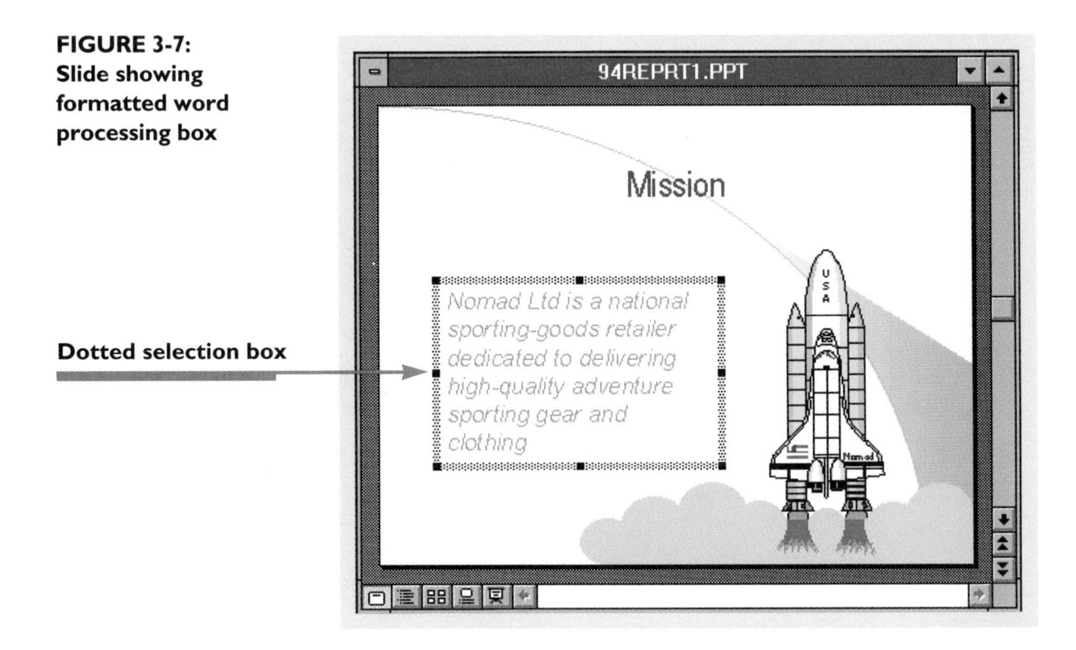

QUICK TIP

The size of your slide text should be set no lower than 18 points to be easily read by your audience.

Drawing and modifying objects

PowerPoint's drawing capabilities allow you to draw and modify lines, shapes, and pictures to enhance your presentation. Table 3-2 describes several drawing methods. Similar to the text objects you learned about in Unit 2, lines and shapes that you create with the PowerPoint drawing tools are objects that you can change and manipulate at any time. PowerPoint shapes and lines have graphic attributes, such as fill color, fill pattern, line color, line style, and shadow that you can change. ▶ Follow Lynn as she rearranges a text object on Slide 4 of the president's presentation and then draws an object to enhance the look of the slide.

1 **Press [Shift] then click the main text object**
A dotted selection box with small black boxes called **resize handles** appears around the text object. The resize handles let you adjust the size and shape of the object. Lynn reduces the text object so it takes up less room.

2 **Position the pointer over the right middle resize handle, then drag the resize handle to the left until the text object is about half its original size**
When you drag a text object's resize handle, the pointer changes to +, and an outline of the text object appears. Lynn is now ready to add a shape.

3 **Click the AutoShapes button on the Drawing toolbar, click the Thick Up Arrow Tool button on the AutoShapes toolbar, then click the AutoShapes toolbar control menu box**
Figure 3-8 shows the AutoShapes toolbar. When you select a shape, the pointer changes to +.

4 **Position the pointer in the blank area of the slide to the right of the text object, press [Shift], drag down and to the right to create an arrow shape similar to the one shown in Figure 3-9, then release the mouse button**
When you release the mouse button, the arrow assumes its position on the slide, filled with a default color. You can use the **adjustment handle**, shown in Figure 3-9, to change the dimensions of an object. Lynn decides to add the Drawing+ toolbar to her window and change the line width of the arrow. If the Drawing+ toolbar is already on your screen, skip Step 5 and continue with Step 6.

5 **Click View on the menu bar, click Toolbars, click the Drawing+ toolbar check box to select it, then click OK**
The Drawing+ toolbar appears on your screen.

6 **Click the Line Style button on the Drawing+ toolbar, then click the third line style down from the top**
PowerPoint applies the new line style to the arrow. Now, hide the Drawing+ toolbar forthe next student, and continue to the next lesson to see how Lynn edits the arrow shape to fit the design of the slide.

7 **Click View on the menu bar, click Toolbars, click the Drawing+ toolbar check box to deselect it, then click OK**

FIGURE 3-8: AutoShapes toolbar

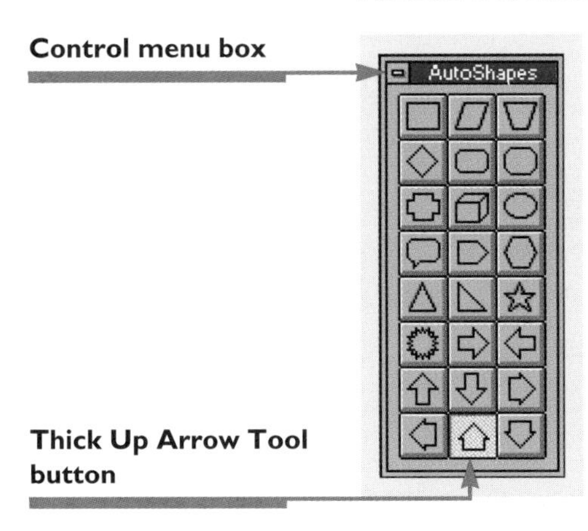

FIGURE 3-9: Slide showing arrow object

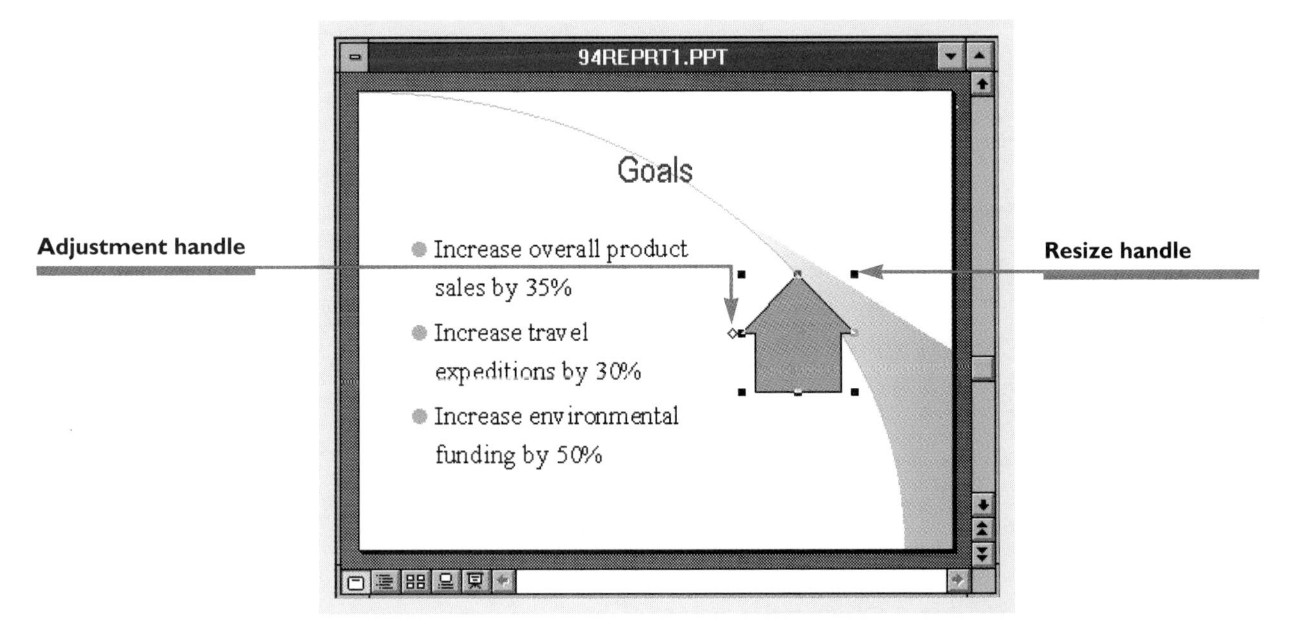

TABLE 3-2: Drawing methods

METHOD	EXAMPLE
Click any drawing tool then drag to create an unproportional object	rectangle, ellipse
Click any drawing tool, press [Shift], then drag to create a proportional object from the edge of the object	square, circle
Click any drawing tool, press [Ctrl], then drag to create a proportional object from the center of the object	square, circle

QUICK TIP

To quickly add or hide a toolbar, position the pointer over a toolbar, click the right mouse button, then click the toolbar you want to add or hide from the menu.

Editing objects

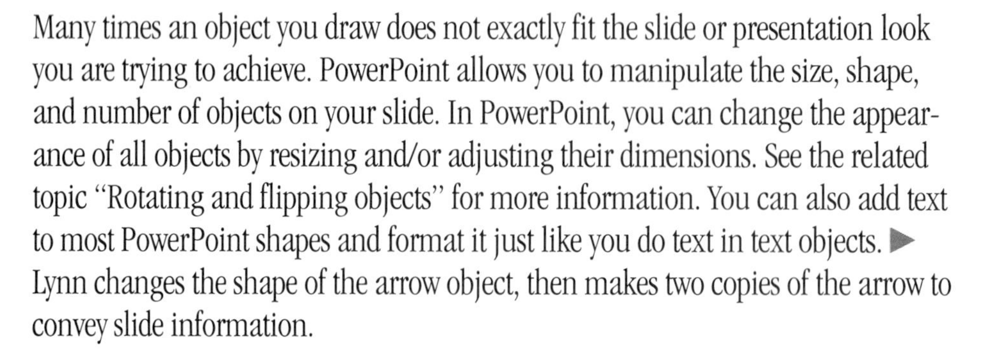

Many times an object you draw does not exactly fit the slide or presentation look you are trying to achieve. PowerPoint allows you to manipulate the size, shape, and number of objects on your slide. In PowerPoint, you can change the appearance of all objects by resizing and/or adjusting their dimensions. See the related topic "Rotating and flipping objects" for more information. You can also add text to most PowerPoint shapes and format it just like you do text in text objects. ▶ Lynn changes the shape of the arrow object, then makes two copies of the arrow to convey slide information.

1. **If the arrow object is not selected, click it**
2. **Drag the bottom middle resize handle up about ½"**
   The size and shape of your arrow should look similar to the arrow object in Figure 3-10. Lynn is satisfied with the way the arrow looks, so she decides to move the arrow into place on the slide.
3. **Drag the arrow up so it assumes the position of the arrow shown in Figure 3-10**
   An outline appears when you move the arrow object to help you position it in the correct place. Now, Lynn makes two copies of her arrow object and places them below the first object.
4. **Position the pointer over the arrow object, then press and hold [Ctrl]**
   Notice that a plus sign (+) appears next to the pointer indicating that PowerPoint will make a copy of the arrow object when you drag the pointer.
5. **Drag a copy of the arrow object down the slide so it assumes a position similar to the second arrow object in Figure 3-11, then release the mouse button**
   An exact copy of the first arrow object, including all graphic and text attributes, is made. Lynn makes a copy of the second arrow object.
6. **Press [Ctrl], drag a copy of the arrow object down the slide, then release the mouse button**
   Compare your screen to Figure 3-11. Lynn now adds some text to her arrow objects.
7. **Double-click the top arrow object, then type 35%**
   An insertion point appears in the arrow object, which indicates it is ready to accept text. The text appears in the center of the object. Now, add text to the other two arrow objects.
8. **Double-click the middle arrow object, then type 30%; double-click the bottom arrow object, type 50%, then click a blank area of the slide to deselect the object**
   In the next lesson, Lynn aligns and groups the arrow objects and then copies them to a different slide.

FIGURE 3-10: Slide showing resized arrow object

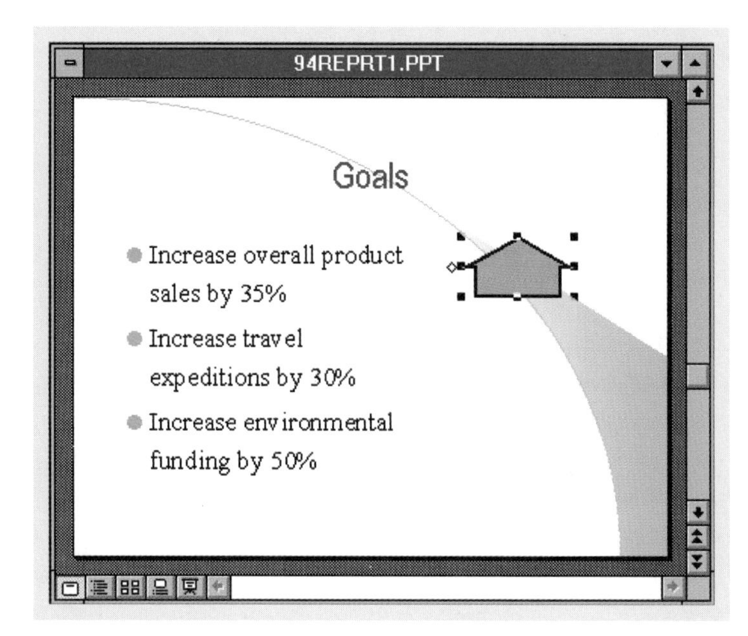

FIGURE 3-11: Slide showing arrow objects

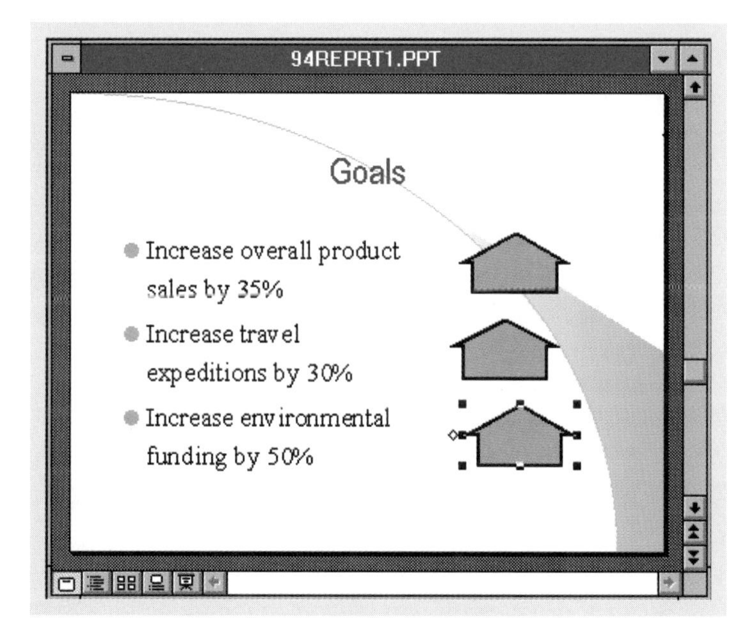

Rotating and flipping objects

Another way to change the appearance of an object is to rotate or flip it. To rotate or flip an object, select it, click Draw on the menu bar, click Rotate/Flip, then click one of the available menu commands, as shown in Figure 3-12.

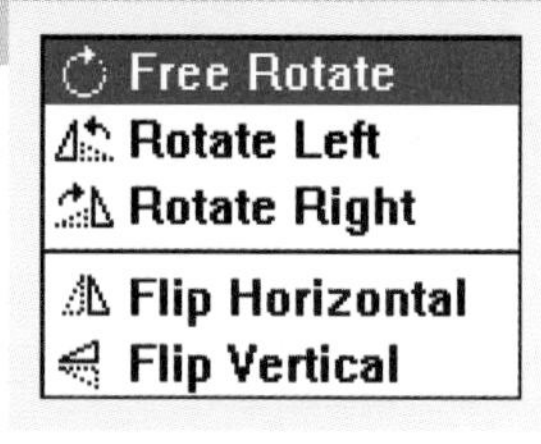

FIGURE 3-12: Rotate/Flip cascading menu

QUICK TIP

Be careful not to put too much information (text or graphics) on one slide. If possible, keep your slide text to 25 words or less.

Aligning and grouping objects

After you create your objects, modify their appearance, and edit their shape and size, you can position them on the slide by aligning and grouping common objects together. The Align command aligns objects relative to each other by snapping the selected objects to an invisible grid of evenly spaced vertical or horizontal lines. You can also group objects into one object to make editing and moving much easier. In PowerPoint you can group, ungroup, or regroup objects. You can also position objects on top of each other. See the related topic "Object stacking order" for more information. ▶ Lynn aligns and groups the arrow objects and then copies and pastes the grouped object to the next slide.

1 Press **[Shift]** then click **each arrow object** to select all three
Lynn decides to leave the objects where they are on the slide but align them together vertically.

2 Click **Draw** on the menu bar, then click **Align**
A list of alignment options appears. The top three options align objects vertically, while the bottom three align objects horizontally. Lynn decides to align the arrow objects to their center.

3 Click **Centers**
The arrow objects align themselves to the center, as shown in Figure 3-13. Now, Lynn groups the objects together to maintain their exact spacing and position relative to each other.

4 Click **Draw** on the menu bar, then click **Group**
The arrow objects group together to form one object without losing their individual attributes. You can ungroup objects to restore each individual object. Lynn likes the arrow objects and decides to make a copy of them and paste them on the next slide.

5 Click the **arrow object** with the right mouse button
A shortcut menu opens, giving you access to common object commands.

6 Click **Copy** in the shortcut menu, then click the **Next Slide button**
The arrow object is copied to the Clipboard, and Slide 5 appears.

7 Click the **Paste button** on the Standard toolbar
The arrow object appears on Slide 5. Notice that the position of the pasted arrow object is the same as it was on Slide 4. Now, Lynn needs to change the text in the arrow objects to match the slide text.

8 Double-click the **top arrow object**, then type **53.4%**; double-click the **middle arrow object**, then type **26.9%**; double-click the **bottom arrow object**, type **6.3%**, then click outside the object to deselect it
Compare your screen to Figure 3-14.

FIGURE 3-13: Slide showing aligned arrow objects

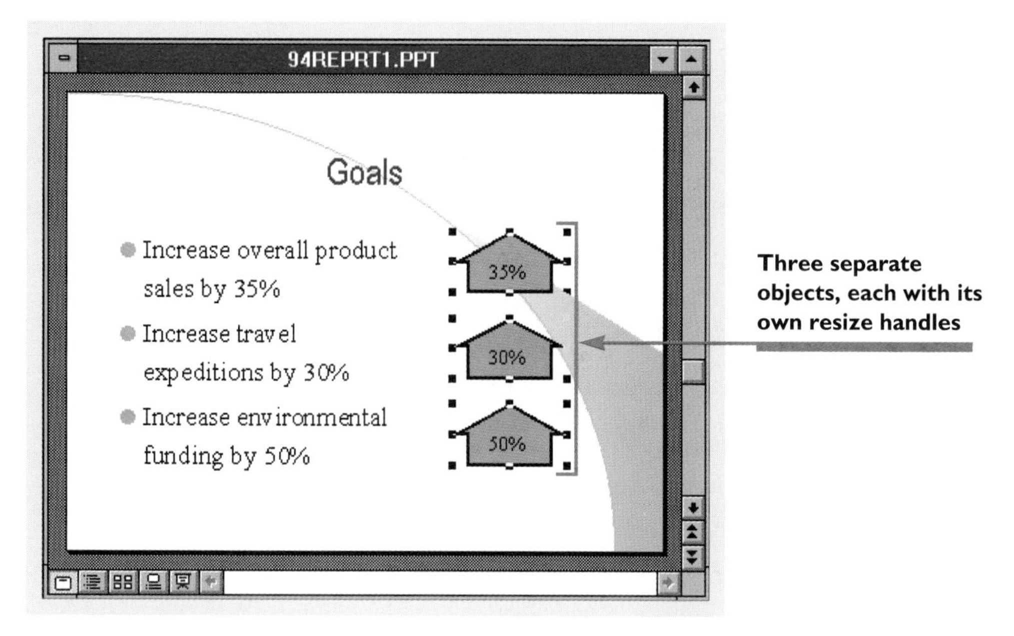

FIGURE 3-14: Slide 5 showing pasted arrow objects

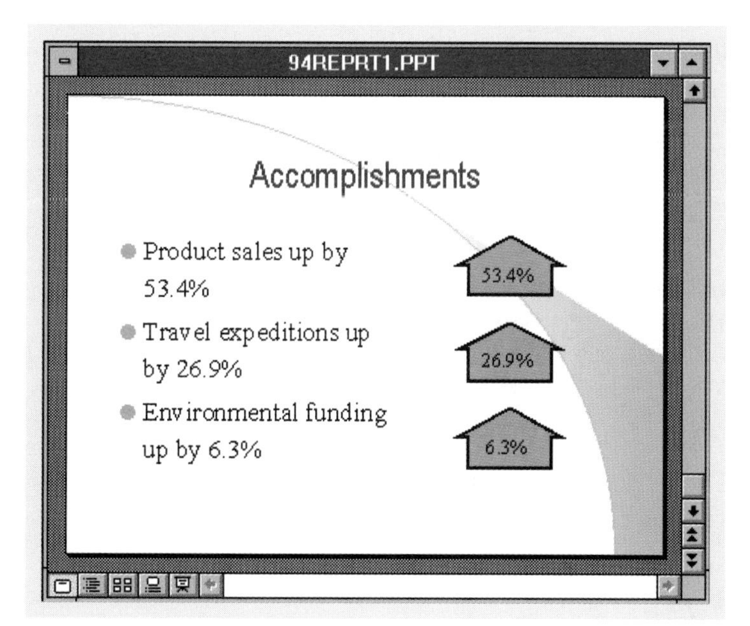

Object stacking order

A **stacking order** is how objects are placed on one another. The first object you draw is on the bottom of the stack. The last object you draw is on the top of the stack. You can change the order of the stack by using the Bring to Front, Send to Back, Bring Forward, and Send Backward commands located on the Draw menu. The stacking order of objects is important to know when you are working with layers of objects to achieve a certain look.

TROUBLE?

If the copy command on the shortcut menu is dimmed when you click the arrow object, move your pointer over the colored area of one of the arrows, not on the text, then click the right mouse button.

Replacing text

As you review your presentation, there might be certain words or fonts that you want to change or replace throughout the entire presentation. In PowerPoint, you can find and replace text case attributes, periods, words or sentences, and fonts. See the related topic "Changing text case and periods" for more information. ▶ Upon review of her work, Lynn decides to replace the slide title font and text.

1 Click **Tools** on the menu bar, then click **Replace Fonts**
The Replace Font dialog box opens. If text is selected before you open the Replace Font dialog box, the font used in the selected text appears in the Replace list box. If no text is selected, the font currently listed on the Formatting toolbar appears in the Replace list box.

2 Click the **Replace list arrow**, then click **Arial Narrow**
Arial Narrow, the font you want to replace, appears in the Replace list box.

3 Click the **With list arrow**, scroll the list if necessary, then click **Arial**
Compare your dialog box to Figure 3-15. PowerPoint will replace all of the Arial Narrow title text in your presentation with Arial when you click the Replace button.

4 Click **Replace** then click **Close**
PowerPoint replaces the title font and then closes the Replace Font dialog box. Now Lynn wants to change the word "Accomplishments" to "Achievements" throughout the presentation.

5 Click **Edit** on the menu bar, then click **Replace**
The Replace dialog box opens and displays the insertion point in the Find What text box, as shown in Figure 3-16.

6 Type **Accomplishments** then press **[Tab]**
Pressing [Tab] moves the insertion point to the Replace With text box. Now, type in the new word.

7 Type **Achievements** then click **Replace All**
PowerPoint replaces the word "Accomplishments" with "Achievements" in all views of your presentation.

8 Click **Close** then click the **Selection Tool button** on the Drawing toolbar
The Replace dialog box closes, and the title is deselected. Compare your screen to Figure 3-17.

FIGURE 3-15: Replace Font dialog box

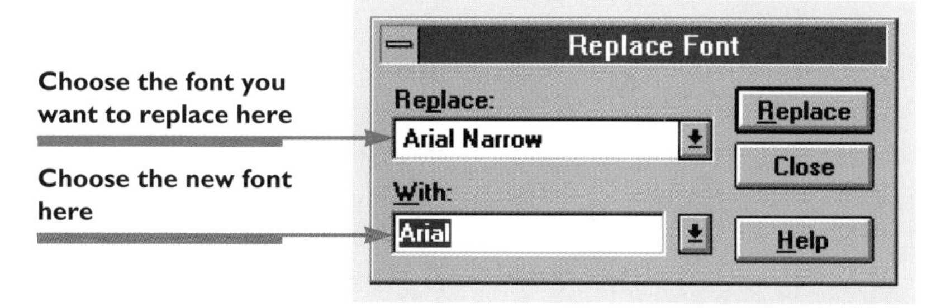

FIGURE 3-16: Replace dialog box

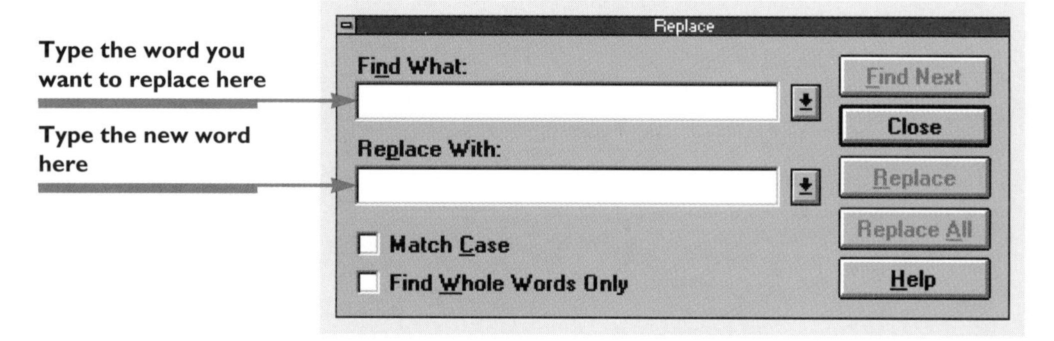

FIGURE 3-17: Slide with replaced title text

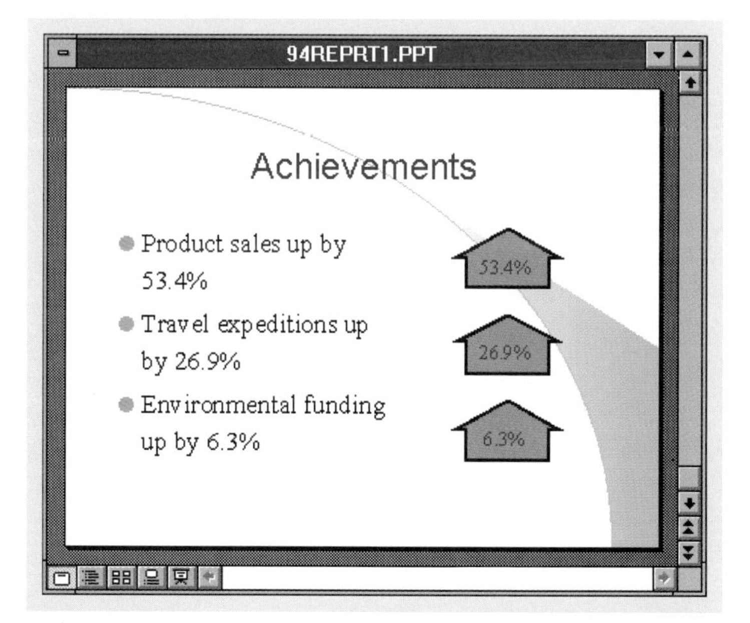

Changing text case and periods

Sometimes it is useful to change the text case of certain words or sentences in your presentation. Select the text object, click Format on the menu bar, then click Change Case to access all the text case options. PowerPoint also has a command to add or remove periods. If you add periods, PowerPoint places periods at the end of each sentence in your presentation. Click Format on the menu bar, then click Periods to access the Period dialog box.

Checking spelling

As your work nears completion, you need to review and proofread your presentation thoroughly for errors. You can check for spelling errors using PowerPoint's spell checker, but it is still important that you proofread it for punctuation and word usage errors. PowerPoint's spell checker recognizes misspelled words, not misused words. For example, the spell checker would not detect The Test even if you intended to type The Best. ▶ Lynn is finished adding and changing text in the presentation, so she checks the spelling.

1. **Click the Spelling button** on the Standard toolbar
   PowerPoint begins to check spelling. When PowerPoint finds a misspelled word or a word it doesn't recognize, the Spelling dialog box opens, as shown in Figure 3-18. In this case, PowerPoint does not recognize the president's last name on Slide 1 (if you made a typing error, another word might appear in this dialog box). Lynn knows the word is spelled correctly so she tells PowerPoint to ignore the word and continue through the presentation. You could also add this word to the dictionary so PowerPoint won't consider it misspelled. See the related topic "Adding words to the Custom dictionary" for more information.

2. Click **Ignore**
   The spell checker ignores the word. The spell checker finds the misspelled word "Outdor" on the same slide. Lynn doesn't want to ignore this word so she fixes the spelling.

3. Click **Outdoor** in the Suggestions list box, then click **Change**
   PowerPoint replaces the incorrect word and continues checking the presentation.

4. Continue checking the spelling in your presentation
   If PowerPoint finds another word it does not recognize, either change it or ignore it. When the spell checker is done checking your presentation, a Microsoft PowerPoint dialog box opens, indicating the spell checker is finished.

5. Click **OK**
   The dialog box closes.

6. Click **File** on the menu bar, click **Close**, then click **Yes** in the dialog box

7. Exit the application

FIGURE 3-18: Spelling dialog box

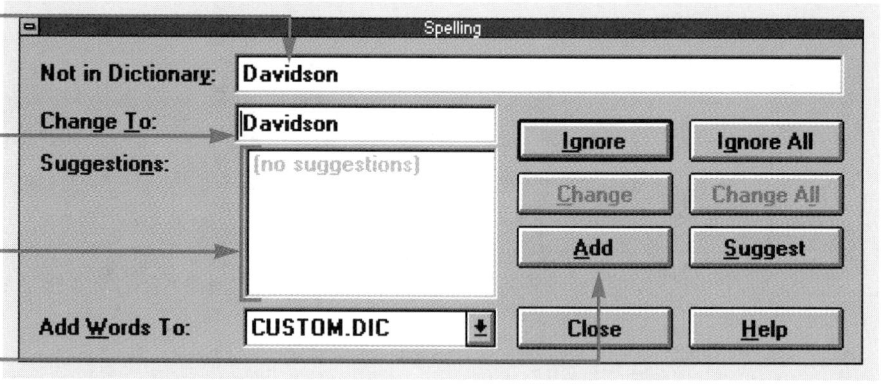

Unrecognized word appears here

Suggested replacement appears here

Alternatives appear here

Click to add words to Custom dictionary

Spelling

Not in Dictionary: Davidson

Change To: Davidson

Suggestions: (no suggestions)

Add Words To: CUSTOM.DIC

Ignore | Ignore All | Change | Change All | Add | Suggest | Close | Help

Adding words to the Custom dictionary

If there is a word you use all the time that is not included in PowerPoint's dictionary, add the word to the Custom dictionary by clicking Add in the Spelling dialog box when PowerPoint suggests the word is misspelled.

QUICK TIP

The PowerPoint spell checker does not check the text in pictures or embedded objects. You'll need to spell check text in imported objects using their original application.

CONCEPTSREVIEW

Label each of the elements of the PowerPoint window shown in Figure 3-19.

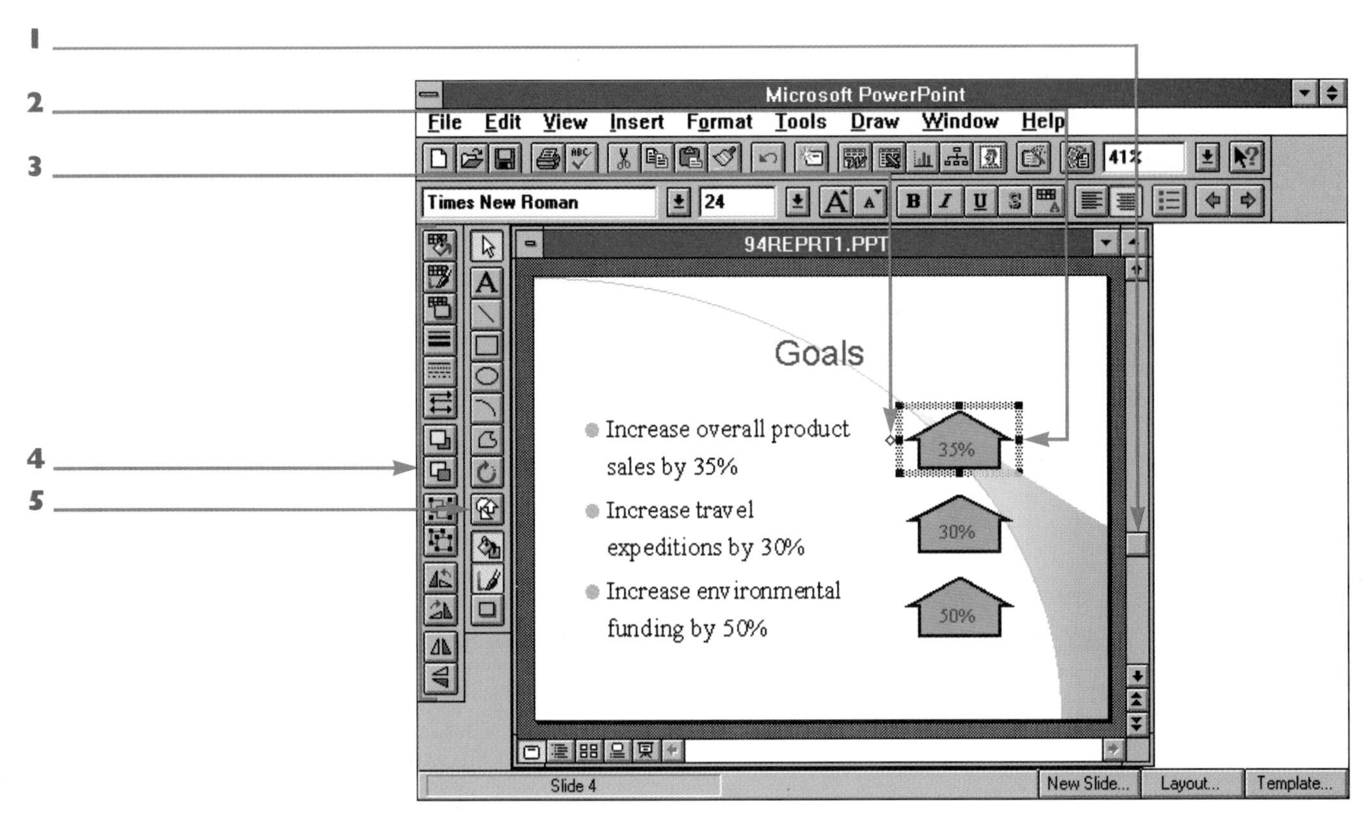

FIGURE 3-19

Match each of the terms with the statement that describes its function.

6 Turns a feature on and off

7 Use this to create a text object on a slide

8 Small box used to move between slides in the vertical scroll bar

9 A text object that does not word wrap

10 A text object you create by dragging a box with the Text tool

a. Elevator
b. Text label
c. Word processing box
d. Text tool
e. Toggle button

Select the best answer from the list of choices.

11 Saving a presentation using the Save As command
a. Opens a blank presentation
b. Saves a copy of the original presentation with a new name
c. Saves the original presentation
d. No different than the Save command

12 What objects can you create with the Text tool?
a. Text placeholder and text object
b. Word placeholder and text box
c. Text label and word processing box
d. Word processing label and text placeholder

13 You know a whole object is selected and can be moved when
a. A slanted line selection box with resize handles appears
b. An outline of the object appears
c. An object selection box appears
d. A dotted line selection box with resize handles appears

14 How do you change the shape of a PowerPoint object?
a. Move the size handle.
b. Move the resize button.
c. Move the adjustment handle.
d. You can't change the shape of a PowerPoint object.

15 All of the following statements about objects are true, EXCEPT:

a. You can add text to all objects.

b. You can resize the shape of objects.

c. You can adjust the dimension of an object.

d. You can copy and paste objects to different slides.

APPLICATIONS REVIEW

1 Open an existing presentation and save it with a new name.

a. Start PowerPoint from the Program Manager window.

b. Click the Blank Presentation radio button or click the Open button on the Standard toolbar.

c. Click the Drives list arrow, then select the drive containing your Student Disk.

d. Click UNIT_3-2.PPT in the File Name list box, then click OK.

e. Click File on the menu bar, then click Save As.

f. Click the Drives list arrow, then select the MY_FILES directory on your Student Disk.

g. Select the current filename, type PROGRESS in the File Name text box, then click OK. Click OK in the Summary Info box, if necessary.

2 Add a word processing box and arrange text.

a. Move to Slide 2 and click the Text Tool button on the Drawing toolbar.

b. Position the pointer near the bottom of the slide, then drag to create a box about 3" wide.

c. Type "Department product managers have 20 min. for line reports."

d. Double-click the word "product," then move it in front of the word "line."

e. Deselect the object.

3 Format text.

a. Press [Shift], then click the word processing box you just created to select it.

b. Click the Italic button on the Formatting toolbar to turn the italic attribute off.

c. Use the Text Color button on the Formatting toolbar to change the color of the text to red.

d. Use the Center Alignment button on the Formatting toolbar to center the text and then deselect the word processing box.

4 Draw and modify an object.

a. Move to Slide 3. If the AutoShapes toolbar is already visible, skip Step b.

b. Click the AutoShapes button on the Drawing toolbar.

c. Click the Seal Tool button on the AutoShapes toolbar, then hide the AutoShapes toolbar.

d. Position the pointer in the lower-right corner of the slide.

e. Press [Shift], then drag to create a seal shape about 1½" wide. Add the Drawing+ toolbar to your screen to change the shape attributes.

f. If the Drawing+ toolbar is not visible on your screen, move the pointer over a toolbar, click the right mouse button, then click Drawing+ in the shortcut menu.

g. Click the Fill Color button on the Drawing+ toolbar, then click the blue color cell.

h. Click the Line On/Off button and the Shadow On/Off button on the Drawing+ toolbar, then deselect the object.

i. Hide the Drawing+ toolbar.

5 Edit the shape and add text to objects.

a. Move to Slide 4 then click the arrow shape to select it.

b. Drag the right middle resize handle to the left about 1".

c. Drag the adjustment handle slightly to the right to change the shape of the arrow tip. Compare your arrow object to the arrows in Figure 3-20.

d. Make two copies of the arrow object by pressing [Ctrl] and dragging the arrow object. Try to put an even amount of space between the objects, as shown in Figure 3-20.

e. Double-click the left arrow object, then type "Teams"; double-click the middle arrow object, then type "Goals"; double-click the right arrow object, then type "Resources"; double-click the cube, type "OutBack," press [Enter], then type "Product."

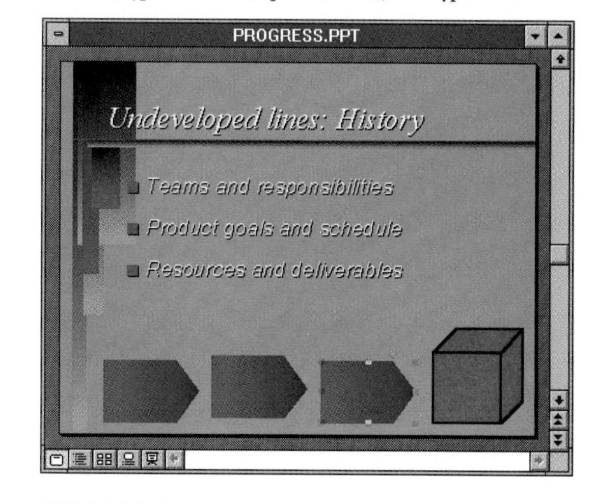

FIGURE 3-20

6 Align and group objects.

a. Select all of the objects using the Shift key.

b. Click Draw on the menu bar, then click Align.

c. Click Bottoms in the list.

d. Click Draw on the menu bar, then click Group.

e. Press [Up Arrow] twice to move the grouped object.

7 Check spelling.

a. Click the Spelling button on the Standard toolbar. The Spelling dialog box opens and begins to check the spelling of the presentation.

b. Fix the misspelled word "Acomplishments," then continue through the presentation. The spell checker will stop on all words it doesn't recognize.

c. When the spell checker finishes, click the Save button on the Standard toolbar, then click File on the menu bar.

d. Print the presentation in Slide view and then close the presentation and exit PowerPoint.

INDEPENDENT CHALLENGE 1

The ABC Learning Company is a Silicon Valley-based corporation dedicated to the design and development of children's instructional software. As the company's main graphics designer, the marketing manager has asked you to design and develop a standardized set of graphics for the company that all the employeesccan use for their business presentations. To help promote the company, the marketing group unveiled a new company slogan: "Learning is easy as ABC."

Plan and create standard text and graphical objects for the ABC Learning Company that employees can copy and paste into their business presentations. Create three different slides with a company logo using the AutoShapes toolbar and a company slogan using the Text tool. The marketing group will decide which of the three designs looks best. Create your own presentation slides, but assume the following: the company colors are blue and red (from the default PowerPoint color scheme).

To complete this independent challenge:

1 Think about the results you want to see, the information you need to create this presentation, and the type of message you want to communicate.

2 Sketch a sample presentation on a piece of paper, indicating the presentation look and the layout of the information. What text and graphics are needed for the slides?

3 Create a new presentation by using the Blank Presentation option and choosing the Blank AutoLayout. Remember you are creating and entering your own presentation material. The logo and the marketing slogan should look good together and the logo objects should be grouped together to make it easier for other employees to copy and paste.

4 Save the presentation as ABCLRNNG.PPT in MY_FILES directory on your Student Disk. Before printing, look through the slides so you know what the presentation will look like. Adjust any items as needed, and print the slides.

5 Submit your presentation plan, preliminary sketches, and the final presentation printout.

INDEPENDENT CHALLENGE 2

You are the construction foreman for Zimmerman Engineering, a civil engineering and construction firm. One of your responsibilities is to create a process flow diagram for the construction team to follow during the building of a custom home. The process flow diagram describes the construction process from start to finish.

Plan and create a construction process flow diagram using PowerPoint's text and drawing tools. The diagram should include shapes, lines, and text labels to indicate the flow of information.

Create your own materials, but assume the following: the process includes planning, getting permits, ordering supplies, hiring subcontractors, building stages, and finishing work.

To complete this independent challenge:

1 Think about the results you want to see, the information you need to create this presentation, and the type of message you want to communicate.

2 Sketch a sample presentation on a piece of paper, indicating the presentation look and the layout of the information. What text and graphics are needed for the slides?

3 Create a new presentation by using the Blank Presentation option and choosing the Blank AutoLayout. Remember you are creating and entering your own presentation material. The diagram objects should be grouped together to make it easier for other employees to change.

4 Save the presentation as DIAGRAM.PPT in the MY_FILES directory on your Student Disk. Before printing, look through the slides so you know what the presentation will look like. Adjust any items as needed, and print the slides.

5 Submit your presentation plan, preliminary sketches, and the final presentation printout.

UNIT 4

OBJECTIVES

- Insert clip art
- Insert a graph
- Format a chart
- Work with an organizational chart
- Insert WordArt
- Work with a Slide Master
- Choose a color scheme
- Annotate slides during a slide show
- Use slide show special effects

A PRESENTATION

You already know how to create a presentation, enter and edit text in Slide view and Outline view, and draw and format objects. When you are giving a presentation, it's important to supplement the text on your slides with pictures, graphs, charts, and other visuals that help make your points and keep your slide show interesting. In this unit, you will learn how to insert four of the most common visuals to enhance the shareholders' presentation: a picture, a graph, an organizational chart, and stylized text. These last three objects are **embedded objects**, created in another application. Embedded objects maintain links with their original application for easy editing. ▶ Lynn Shaw needs to enhance the appearance of the Annual Report Executive Summary presentation to make it easier to read and understand by the audience. ▶

Inserting clip art

PowerPoint has over 1000 pieces of professionally designed pictures, called **clip art**, that you can import into your presentation. The clip art is stored in a file index system called a **gallery** that sorts all the clip art into categories. You can access the ClipArt Gallery in one of three ways: by double-clicking a clip art placeholder from an AutoLayout, using the Insert Clip Art button on the Standard toolbar, or choosing Clip Art from the Insert menu. You can modify PowerPoint clip art like other PowerPoint objects; for example, you can change the shape, size, fill, shading, and all other clip art style attributes. ▶ In this lesson, Lynn opens the presentation she has been working on and adds a picture from the ClipArt Gallery to one of the slides.

1. Start PowerPoint and open the presentation UNIT_4-1.PPT from your Student Disk, save it as 94FNLRPT.PPT to the MY_FILES directory on your Student Disk, then click **OK** to close the Summary Info dialog box
2. Click the **Next Slide button**
   Lynn uses PowerPoint's AutoLayout feature to add a piece of clip art to Slide 2.
3. Click the **Layout button** Layout... on the status bar
   The Slide Layout dialog box opens with the Bulleted List AutoLayout selected. Lynn selects the Text and Clip Art AutoLayout, which will keep the text object already on the slide intact and insert a placeholder for the clip art.
4. Click the **Text and Clip Art AutoLayout**, as shown in Figure 4-1, then click **Apply**
   PowerPoint applies the Text and Clip Art AutoLayout to the slide by moving the existing text object to the left and inserting a placeholder, which identifies where the clip art object will be placed on the slide.
5. Double-click the **clip art placeholder**, then click **Yes** if necessary
   The Microsoft ClipArt Gallery dialog box opens. The first time you open the ClipArt Gallery, PowerPoint needs to build and organize the clip art visual index. Click Yes to build the index. Depending on the speed of your computer, building the gallery index could take up to 15 minutes.
6. In the Choose a category to view below section, drag the scroll box to the bottom, then click **Transportation**
   The ClipArt Gallery's Preview box changes to display the available clip art in the Transportation category. If the Transportation category doesn't appear, select a different category.
7. In the Preview box, click the **down scroll arrow** several times, then click the **sailboat** shown in Figure 4-2
   Now that Lynn has selected the clip art she wants, she imports the clip art to her slide. If you don't have a picture of a sailboat in your ClipArt Gallery, select a similar picture.
8. Click **OK**, then click a blank area of the Presentation window to deselect the clip art object
   The picture of the sailboat is placed on the right side of the slide in the AutoLayout.

FIGURE 4-1: Slide Layout dialog box

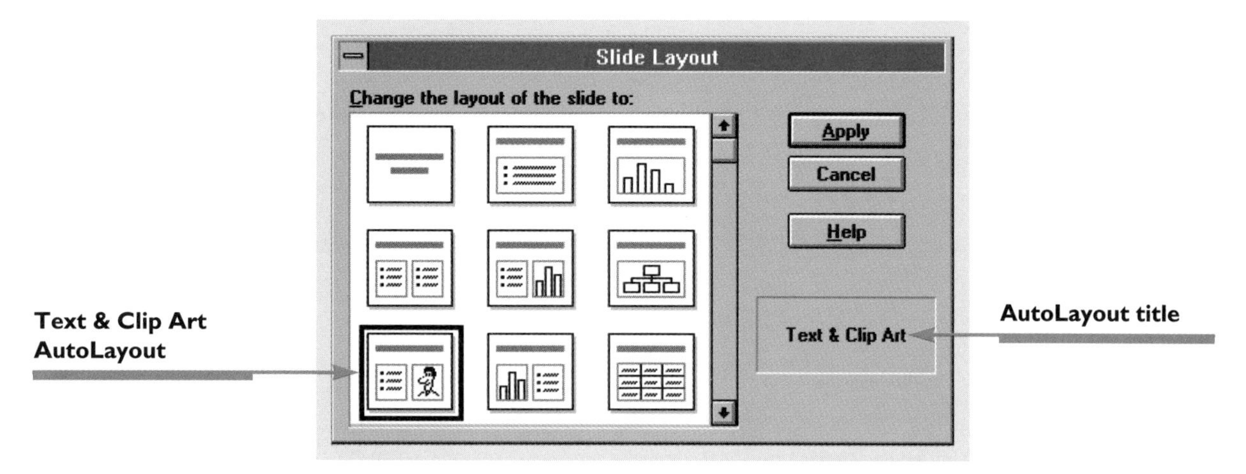

FIGURE 4-2: Microsoft ClipArt Gallery dialog box

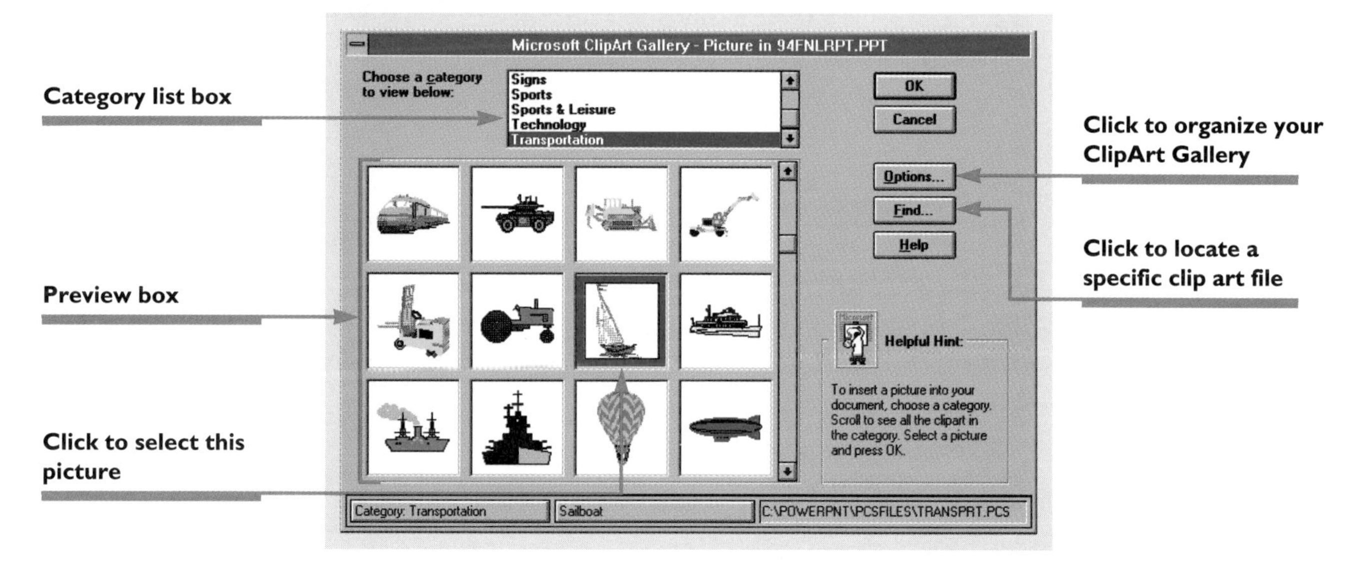

Organizing the ClipArt Gallery

Click the Options button in the Microsoft ClipArt Gallery dialog box to organize your ClipArt Gallery. The Options dialog box opens, letting you add new clip art to the gallery (Add button), rename or delete categories (Change a Category button), and edit the descriptions of the currently selected picture (Edit Picture Information button). Notice in Figure 4-2 that the description of the selected clip art appears on the status bar of the dialog box.

QUICK TIP

Click the Find button in the Microsoft ClipArt Gallery dialog box to locate a specific clip art file. See Figure 4-2.

Inserting a graph

PowerPoint includes an application called Microsoft Graph, referred to as Graph, which you use to create a graph for your slides. A **graph** is made up of two components; a **datasheet**, which contains the information you want to display, and a **chart**, which is the graphical representation of the datasheet. You can create your own graph by entering data into a Graph datasheet or you can import data from a Microsoft Excel worksheet. ▶ Follow Lynn as she imports a Microsoft Excel worksheet containing company revenue information that she needs to make into a PowerPoint graph.

1 **Drag the elevator to Slide 6, click the Layout button** Layout... **, click the Graph AutoLayout (in the upper-right corner of the Slide Layout dialog box), then click Apply**
A graph placeholder replaces the bulleted list on the slide.

2 **Double-click the graph placeholder**
Graph starts and displays a default datasheet and chart. The default datasheet appears with datasheet titles along the top row and left column, such as 1st Qtr and East, and datasheet numbers below and to the right of the titles, such as 20.4 in cell A1 (a **cell** is the intersection of a row and a column). A black selection rectangle appears around a cell, indicating it is an **active cell**—selected and ready to accept data. Notice that the PowerPoint toolbars have been replaced with the Graph toolbars. If the Formatting toolbar doesn't appear, click View on the menu bar, click Toolbars, click the Formatting check box, then click OK.

3 **Click the first cell (upper-left corner) in the datasheet**
This indicates where the imported data will appear in the datasheet.

4 **Click the control box in the upper-left corner of the Datasheet window to select the entire datasheet**
Control boxes are the gray boxes located along the edges of the datasheet, as shown in Figure 4-3. The control boxes label the rows and columns in the datasheet. Clicking a row or column control box selects that entire row or column of data. Table 4-1 describes how to select and move around the datasheet.

5 **Click Edit on the menu bar, click Clear, then click All**
The default datasheet contents are deleted.

6 **Click the Import Data button on the Graph Standard toolbar**
The Import Data dialog box opens.

7 **In the File Name list box, click the worksheet UNIT_4-2.XLS from your Student Disk, click OK, then click any cell to deselect the datasheet**
The Excel data appears in the datasheet displaying Nomad sales data for the last three years. See Figure 4-4. You can click an individual cell and then type to enter data, or double-click an individual cell to edit its contents.

8 **Click the View Datasheet button on the Graph Standard toolbar**
The View Datasheet button toggles the datasheet off and out of view.

9 **Click a blank area of the Presentation window to exit Graph, then click a blank area again to deselect the graph object**
The PowerPoint toolbars and menu appear. Compare your slide to Figure 4-5.

FIGURE 4-3: Datasheet and chart in the PowerPoint window

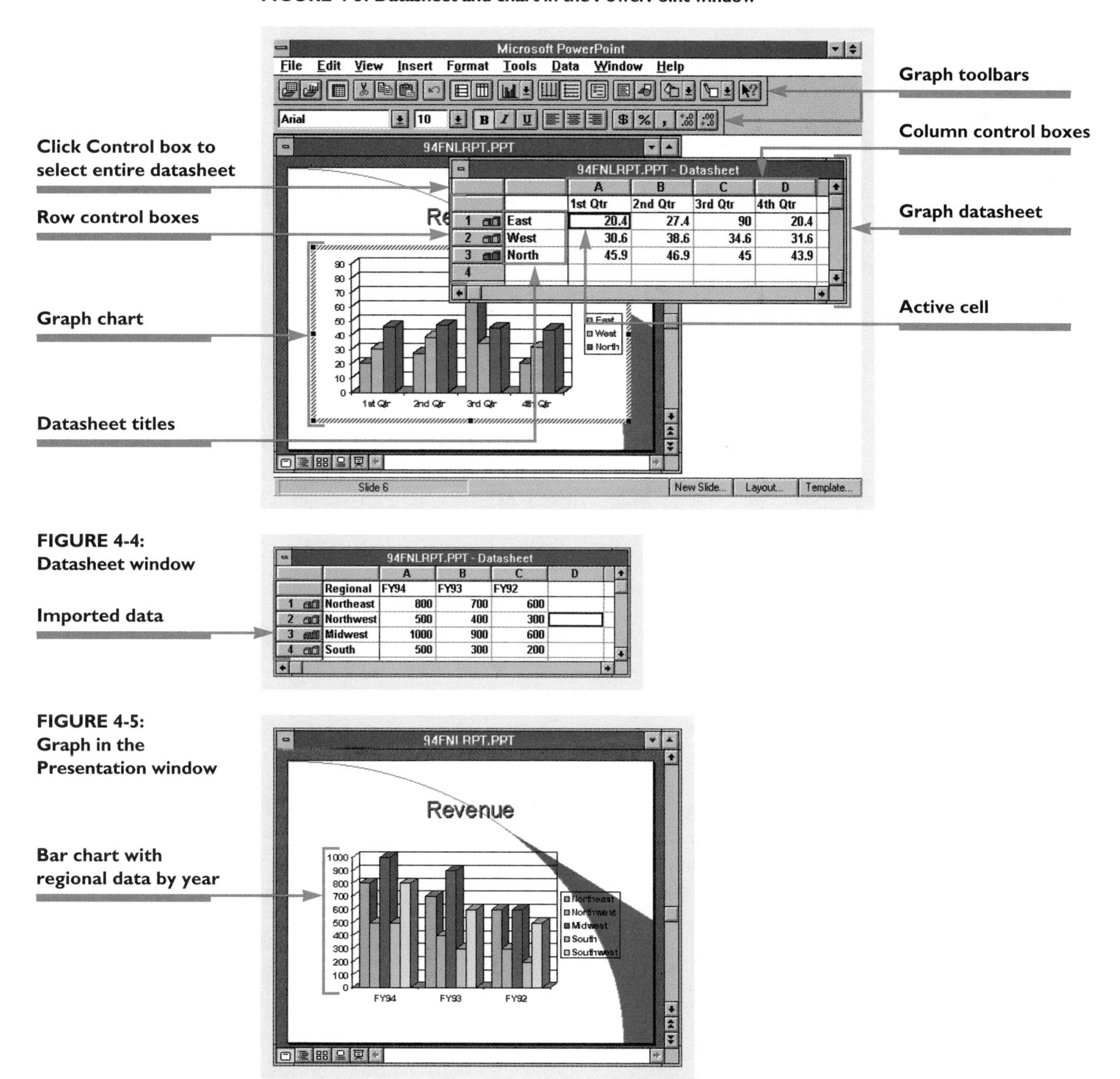

FIGURE 4-4: Datasheet window

FIGURE 4-5: Graph in the Presentation window

TABLE 4-1: Getting around the datasheet

TASK	ACTION
Select a specific cell	Click the specific cell
Select a range of cells	Click the upper-left cell then drag to the lower-right cell of the range
Select a column or row	Click the column or row control box
Select the entire datasheet	Click the upper-left corner control box

TROUBLE?

When the Graph toolbars are present, you are working in Graph. Clicking outside the graph object returns you to the Presentation window.

Formatting a chart

Graph lets you change the appearance of the chart to emphasize certain aspects of the information you are presenting. You can change the way the chart appears, create titles, format the chart labels, move the legend, or add arrows. ▶ Lynn wants to improve the appearance of her chart by displaying the data by region, formatting the x and y axes, and inserting a title.

1. **Double-click the graph object**
   Graph opens and displays Lynn's chart from the previous lesson. The chart currently displays the data by year, FY94, FY93, FY92 (the rows in the datasheet). Lynn wants to change the chart to display the data by region (the columns in the datasheet).
2. **Click the By Column button on the Graph Standard toolbar**
   The chart changes to display the data by region. Now Lynn wants to display the y-axis numbers in currency format with dollar signs ($).
3. **Click the sales numbers on the y-axis, then click the Currency Style button on the Graph Formatting toolbar**
   The sales numbers change to include dollar signs, decimal points, and zeroes. Lynn doesn't like the look of the zeroes to the right of the decimal point so she decides to remove them.
4. **Click the Decrease Decimal button on the Graph Formatting toolbar twice**
   The zeroes to the right of the decimal point are removed from the numbers. Lynn notices that not all the region names are displayed on the x-axis, so she decides to decrease the font size to make sure all the region names fit in the space provided.
5. **Click the region names on the x-axis, click Format on the menu bar, then click Selected Axis**
   The Format Axis dialog box opens, which lets you format the pattern, scale, font, number, or alignment of the selected axis by clicking different tabs in the dialog box.
6. **Click the Font tab, click 14 in the Size list box, as shown in Figure 4-6, then click OK**
   The font size changes from 18 points to 14 points for all the labels on the x-axis. Now Lynn adds a title to the chart.
7. **Click Insert on the menu bar, click Titles, click the Chart Title check box, then click OK**
   A selected text object appears with the word "Title." Lynn enters the chart title.
8. **Type Annual Sales Figures by Region, then click below the chart title**
   If you make a mistake while typing, press [Backspace]. Clicking outside the chart title deselects the title, so you can work on other parts of the graph. After completing the chart, Lynn exits Graph.
9. **Click a blank area of the Presentation window to exit Graph, then click a blank area again to deselect the graph object**
   The PowerPoint toolbars and menu appear. Compare your slide to Figure 4-7. Don't worry if the legend is hard to see. You will correct this later in this Unit.

FIGURE 4-6: Format Axis dialog box

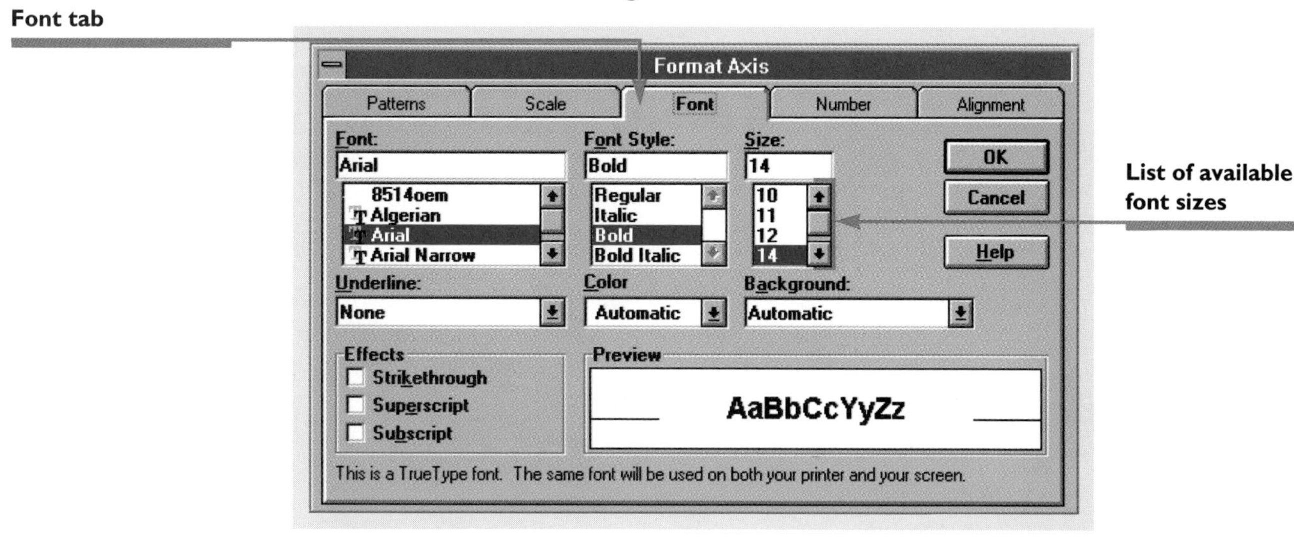

FIGURE 4-7: Slide with chart

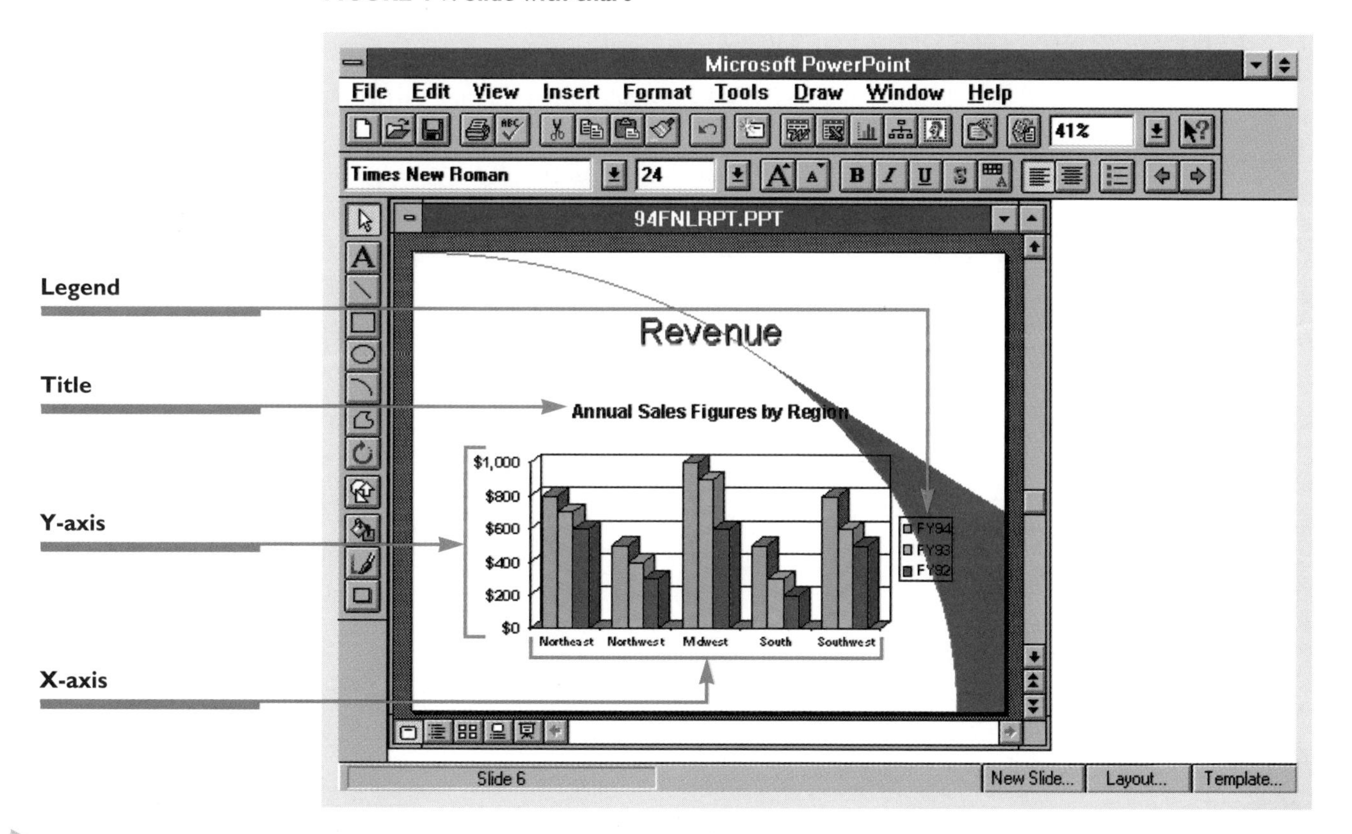

Changing graph formats

You can choose from among a number of formats for your graph. There are 12 graph categories, including two-dimensional graphs and three-dimensional graphs, for a total of 84 different formats. Click the Chart Type list arrow on the Graph Standard toolbar, and then select a chart type, such as Area, Bar, Column, Line, Pie, and Surface, from the list. To change a chart format quickly and easily, use the AutoFormat command on the Format menu.

QUICK TIP

Double-clicking any item in the Graph chart opens an editing dialog box for that item.■

Working with an organizational chart

When you give presentations for the company you work for, often it's helpful to show graphically the organizational structure of your company. An **organizational chart** is a diagram of chart boxes connected together by lines that indicate a company's reporting structure. PowerPoint provides an application called Microsoft Organization Chart that you use to create chart boxes, enter chart text, and format chart boxes. ▶ The current organizational chart for Nomad Ltd needs to be updated since last year's meeting. Lynn adds her name to the current organizational chart.

1. Click the **Next Slide button**
   Slide 7 appears with Nomad's organizational chart from 1994. To edit the organizational chart, double-click the object just as you did with Graph.

2. Double-click the **organizational chart**
   The Nomad Ltd organizational chart appears in a separate window called the Microsoft Organization Chart window.

3. Click the **Microsoft Organization Chart window maximize button**
   The chart from the previous year displays the president's name, Bill Davidson, in a manager chart box. Below that box are four subordinate boxes for the four division officers who report to him. The toolbar offers five different chart box types: subordinate, co-worker (to the right), co-worker (to the left), manager, and assistant. Each of the buttons includes a small chart box with a line indicating the relationship to another chart box. Lynn adds an assistant chart box.

4. Click the **Assistant button** on the Org Chart Standard toolbar, then click the **Bill Davidson chart box**
   A blank assistant chart box appears between the Bill Davidson's chart box and the next level of subordinate chart boxes.

5. Click the **Assistant chart box** you just added
   The blank chart box opens with placeholder text for <Name>, <Title>, <Comment 1>, and <Comment 2>, as shown in Figure 4-8. Lynn enters her name and title in the blank chart box.

6. With <Name> selected type **Lynn Shaw**, press **[Tab]**, type **Executive Assistant**, then click a blank area of the chart window
   Lynn decides to add a shadow to all the chart boxes to enhance the look of the organizational chart.

7. Click **Edit** on the menu bar, click **Select**, then click **All**
   Lynn uses the Select command to quickly and accurately select all the chart boxes.

8. Click **Boxes** on the menu bar, click **Box Shadow**, click the **shadow option** shown in Figure 4-9, then click a blank area of the chart window
   Compare your screen to Figure 4-10. After making all the changes, Lynn exits and returns back to the Presentation window.

9. Click **File** on the menu bar, click **Exit and Return to 94FNLRPT.PPT**, then click **Yes** to update the presentation
   Microsoft Organization Chart updates the PowerPoint slide with the new organizational chart.

FIGURE 4-8: Blank chart box

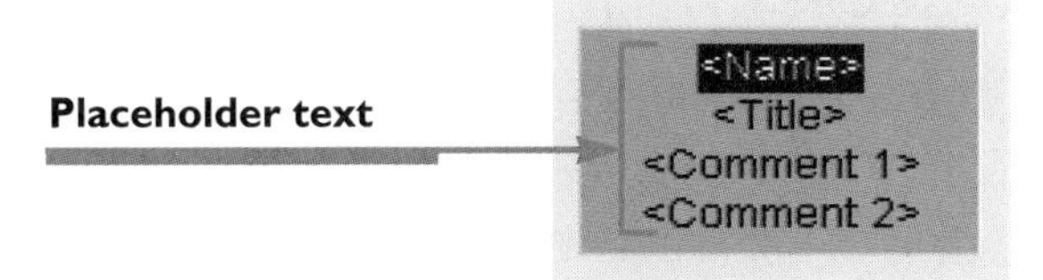

FIGURE 4-9: Box shadow options

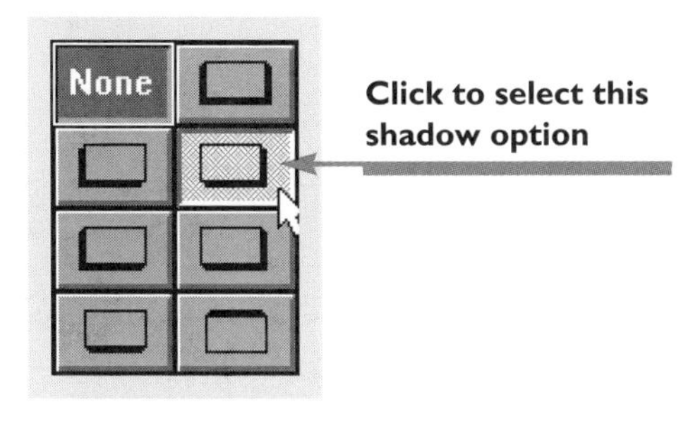

FIGURE 4-10: Slide with new organizational chart

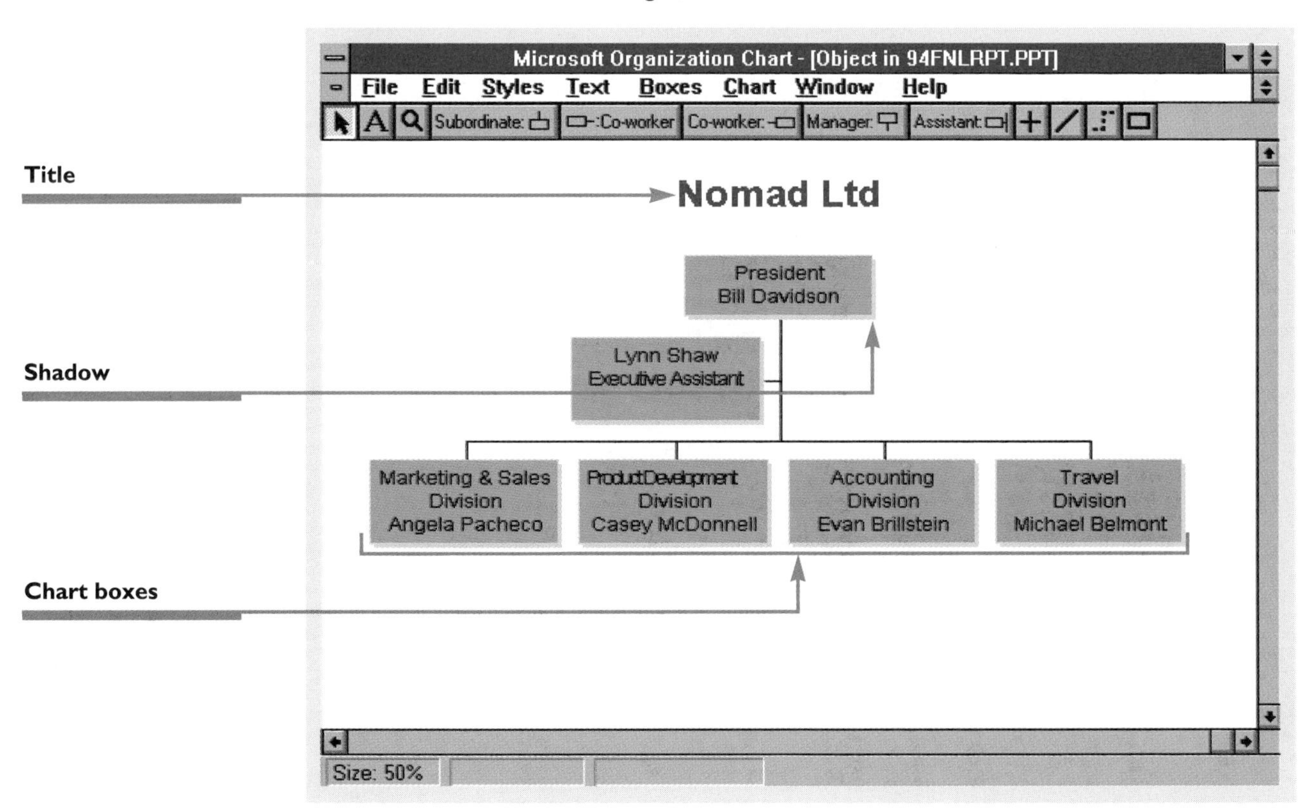

You can move a chart box to a new location by dragging it.

Inserting WordArt

You can insert fancy or stylized text in your presentation with Microsoft WordArt. The objects you create in WordArt are embedded in your slide, and you can move and edit them like other PowerPoint objects. You can format text in a variety of shapes, create unusual alignments, and add 3-D effects using any TrueType font installed on your system. A **TrueType font** is a type of font that can be displayed or printed at any size. ▶ The president wants to end the presentation with a question and answer session. Lynn uses WordArt to enhance the last slide.

1. Click the **Next Slide button**
   Slide 8 appears. Because Lynn is going to place WordArt on this slide, she changes the slide layout to accommodate an object.
2. Click the **Layout button** Layout..., click the **down scroll arrow**, click the **Object AutoLayout**, then click **Apply**
   An object placeholder replaces the bulleted list on the slide.
3. Double-click the **object placeholder**
   The Insert Object dialog box opens, displaying a list of object types, from which Lynn chooses Microsoft WordArt 2.0.
4. In the Object Type list box, click the **down scroll arrow**, click **Microsoft WordArt 2.0**, then click **OK**
   WordArt starts and displays the Enter Your Text Here dialog box with sample text already selected. Notice that the PowerPoint toolbars have been replaced with the WordArt toolbar.
5. Type **Questions**, press **[Enter]**, type **&**, press **[Enter]**, type **Answers**, then click **Update Display**
   The WordArt text appears in the Presentation window. Lynn enhances the text using WordArt's powerful formatting options.
6. Click the **Format Text list arrow** on the WordArt Formatting toolbar, then click the **deflate shape** shown in Figure 4-11
   The text in the window changes to match the selected symbol. Lynn continues by shading the text.
7. Click the **Shading button** on the Formatting toolbar, click the **Foreground list arrow**, click **Fuchsia**, then click **OK**.
   The foreground color of the text changes from black to fuchsia. Lynn decides to add a shadow to the text.
8. Click the **Shadow button** on the Formatting toolbar, then click the **second symbol** in the top row, as shown in Figure 4-12
   A shadow appears behind the text. After completing the text styling, Lynn exits WordArt.
9. Click a blank area of the Presentation window to exit WordArt, then deselect the WordArt object
   The PowerPoint toolbars and menu appear. Compare your screen with Figure 4-13.

FIGURE 4-11:
Format Text list

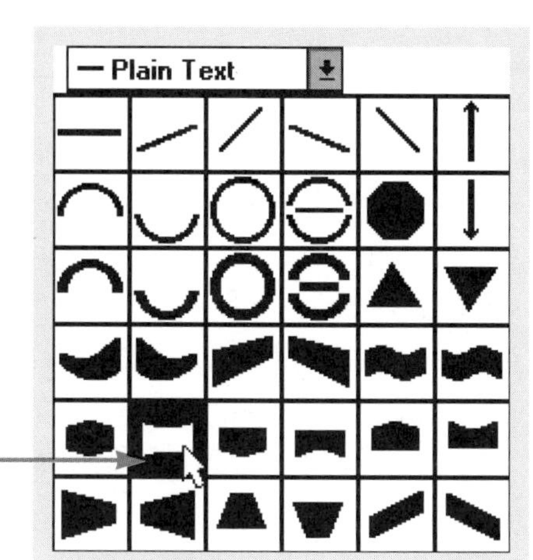

Click to select this shape for the text

FIGURE 4-12:
Shadow list

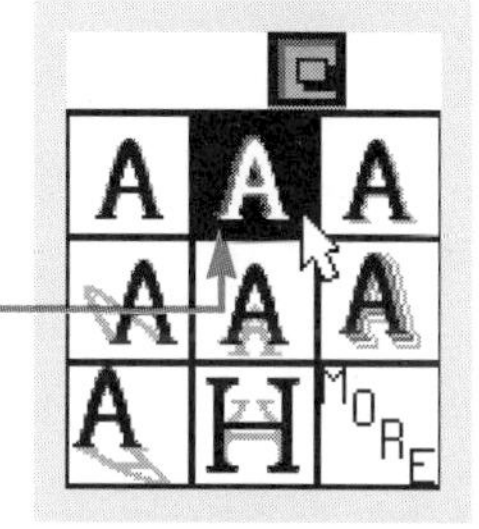

Click to select this text shadow option

FIGURE 4-13:
Slide text enhanced with WordArt

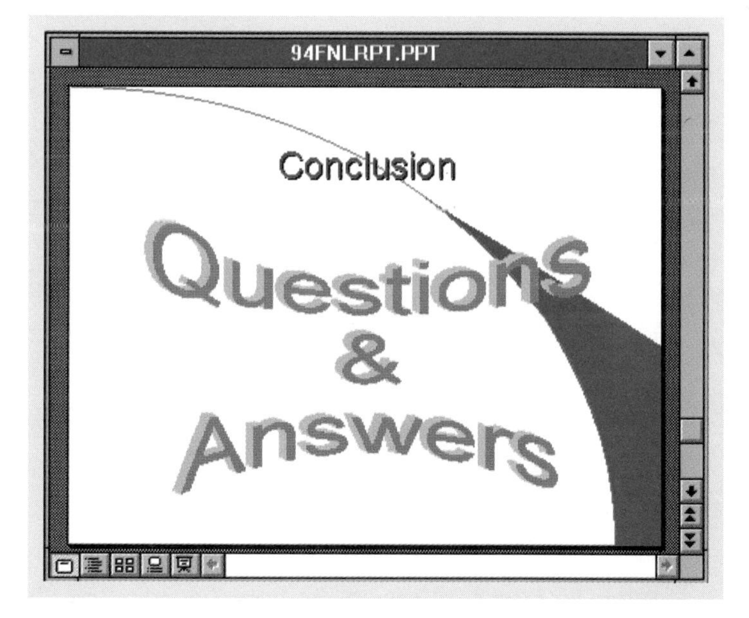

Using other presentation media

Just as you inserted Microsoft WordArt, you can also insert and play sounds and movies during your presentations. From the Insert Object dialog box, click Sound or Media Clip, then click OK. The Sound Recorder or Media Clip dialog box opens. Insert or open a file with the appropriate media type. When you are finished playing or modifying the media, exit back into PowerPoint. For sounds, a small sound icon appears, while for movies, a small screen with the first frame appears on the presentation slide. Use the Play Setting command from the Tools menu to play the sound or movie on a slide or during a slide show.

QUICK TIP

Use the Rotation and Effects command on the WordArt Format menu to add other special effects.■

Working with a Slide Master

PowerPoint uses **masters**, a kind of template for all of the slides in the presentation, to help create consistent and professional-looking slides, audience handouts, and speaker's notes pages. Each PowerPoint view has a corresponding master—Slide Master for Slide view, Notes Master for Notes Pages view, Handout Master for Slide Sorter view, and Outline Master for Outline view. When you add an object or change the text format on a master, the changes appear in each slide in the corresponding view. ▶ Lynn uses the Slide Master to change the bullet type in all her slides and then adds the company's logo to appear in each slide of the presentation.

1. Drag the elevator to Slide 2
   Lynn switches to Slide 2 to make it easier to view her Slide Master changes.
2. Click **View** on the menu bar, click **Master**, then click **Slide Master**
   The status bar changes from Slide 2 to Slide Master. The Slide Master appears with the **master title placeholder** and the **master text placeholder**, as shown in Figure 4-14. The placeholders control the format of the title and main text objects for each slide.
3. Click anywhere in the first line of text in the master text placeholder
   The insertion point appears. PowerPoint applies any change you make to the line of text containing the insertion point to every corresponding line in the presentation. Lynn changes the round bullet on the first line of text to a checkmark.
4. Click **Format** on the menu bar, click **Bullet**, then click the **checkmark**, as shown in Figure 4-15
   This selects the checkmark as the new bullet. Because the size of the previous round bullet is larger than the checkmark, Lynn decides to increase the size of the checkmark from 75% to 100%.
5. Click the **Size % of Text up arrow** until the percentage reaches 100, then click **OK**
   The bullet in the first line of text changes from a round bullet to a checkmark. Lynn now inserts the company's logo.
6. Click **Insert** on the menu bar, then click **Picture**
   The Insert Picture dialog box opens.
7. Click **UNIT_4-6.TIF** from the drive your Student Disk is in, then click **OK**
   The Nomad Ltd logo appears on the Slide Master. Lynn decides to move the logo to an open place on the Slide Master.
8. Drag the logo to the upper-left corner of the slide
   The Nomad Ltd logo appears in the Slide Master. Lynn wants to see how the changes to the Slide Master affect her slides.
9. Click the **Slide View button**
   In Slide view, you can see the changes, as shown in Figure 4-16. You can continue to click the Next Slide button to see changes on each slide.

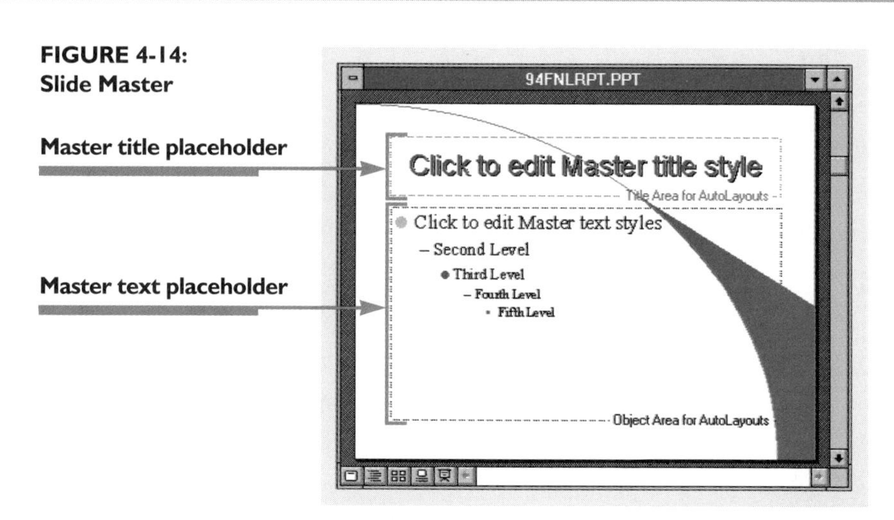

FIGURE 4-14: Slide Master

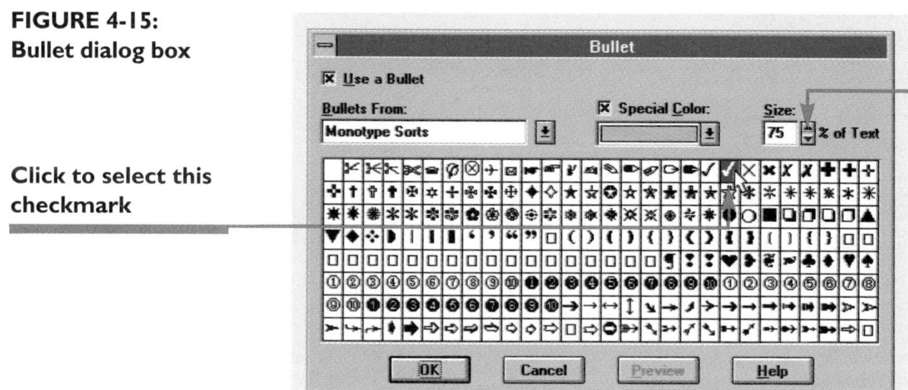

FIGURE 4-15: Bullet dialog box

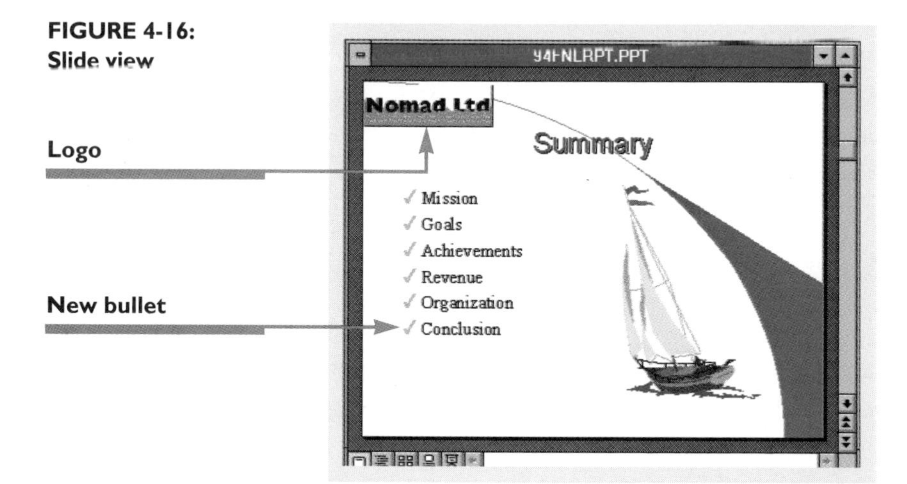

FIGURE 4-16: Slide view

Scaling and cropping pictures

When you insert a picture, sometimes you need to scale or crop the picture to create a desired look. **Scaling** means resizing a picture or object by a certain percentage. You can either use the resize handles on each corner of an object or the Scale command, which lets you resize an object mathematically instead of dragging its resize handles. Sometimes you only need a portion of a picture in your presentation. With the Crop Picture command, you can drag a resize handle using the Cropping tool to cover portions of a picture so you don't see all of it on the screen.

QUICK TIP

Press and hold [Shift] then click a view button to switch to the corresponding master.

Choosing a color scheme

PowerPoint uses sets of eight professionally balanced colors called **color schemes** to help you take the guess work out of deciding which colors look good together. The color schemes determine the main colors in your presentation for slide background, text and lines, title text, shadows, fills, and accents. See Table 4-2 for color descriptions. You can create your own professional looking color schemes using the combinations of colors suggested by the Choose Scheme dialog box. You can also reuse color schemes without having to re-create them. See the related topic "Copying color schemes" for more information. ▶ The president wants to give an on-screen presentation, so Lynn decides to change the color scheme and add a shaded background to enhance the presentation for the screen.

1. **Click Format on the menu bar, then click Slide Color Scheme**
   The Slide Color Scheme dialog box opens, displaying the current color scheme. Lynn wants to choose a new color scheme using the Choose Scheme dialog box.
2. Click **Choose Scheme**, click the **Background Color down scroll arrow**, then click the **blue color** at the bottom of the list
   Now the background of all Lynn's slides will be blue. She next selects a complementary text and line color from the list of choices that appears.
3. Click the **white color** in the Text & Line Color list box, then click the **color scheme** in the upper-right corner of the Other Scheme Colors section
   Selecting a text and line color displays a gallery of four alternative color schemes. See Figure 4-17.
4. Click **OK** then click **Apply to All** in the Slide Color Scheme dialog box
   The new color scheme is applied to all the slides in the presentation. To apply the color scheme to the current slide only, you would click Apply. Lynn decides to add a shaded background to all the slides.
5. Click **Format** on the menu bar, then click **Slide Background**
   The Slide Background dialog box opens.
6. In the Shade Styles section, click the **Horizontal radio button**
   The shade style changes to horizontal, and four shade variants appear. Lynn uses the selected shade variant, but she wants a lighter shade.
7. Click the **Light scroll arrow** twice
   The shade variant lightens. Lynn decides to apply the shaded background, as shown in Figure 4-18, to all the slides.
8. Click **Apply to All**, then click the **Previous Slide button** to view the changes
   The new slide background is applied to all the slides in the presentation.

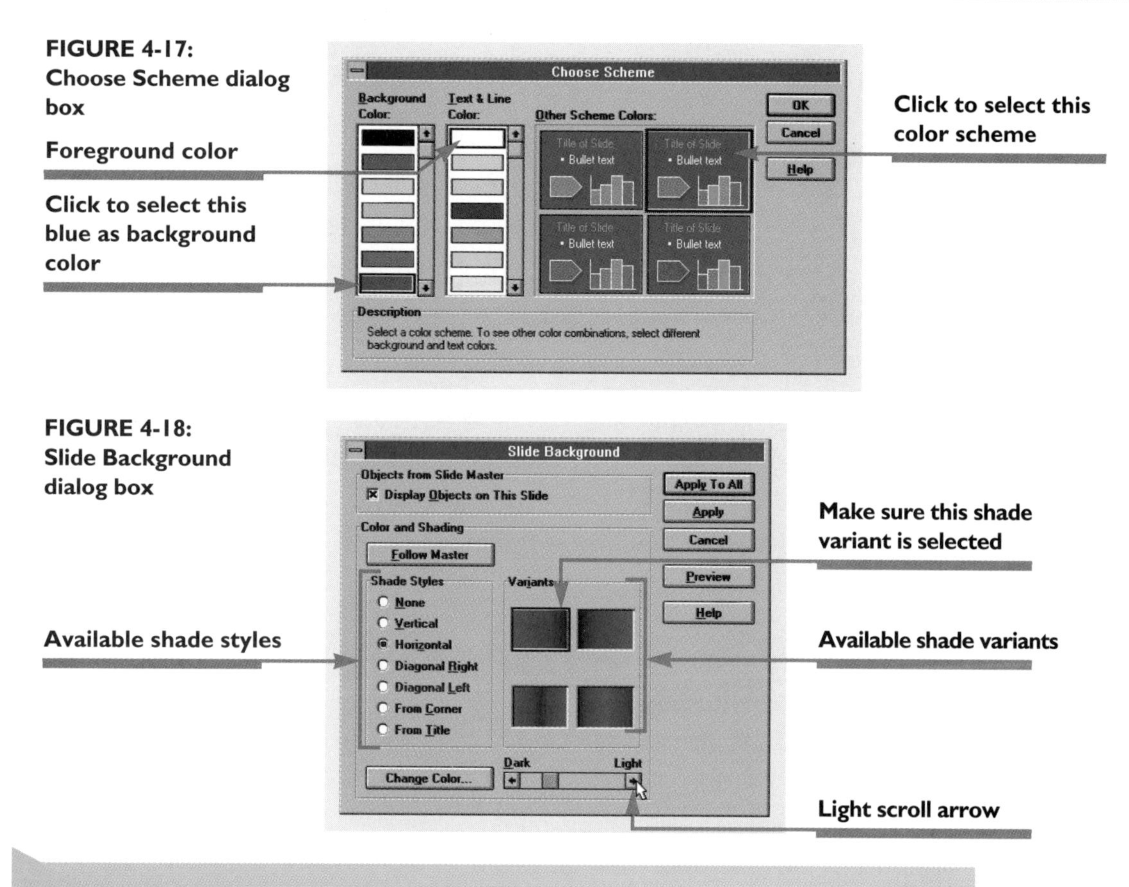

FIGURE 4-17: Choose Scheme dialog box

FIGURE 4-18: Slide Background dialog box

Copying color schemes

You can reuse color schemes without having to re-create them. Simply copy, or pick up, the color scheme from one slide and paste, or apply, the color scheme to another slide. In the Slide Sorter view, select a slide with the color scheme you want to copy, then use the Pick Up Color Scheme command on the Format menu. Select the slide you want to apply the color scheme to in Slide Sorter view from any open presentation, then use the Apply Color Scheme command.

TABLE 4-2: Color schemes

SCHEME COLORS	DESCRIPTION
Background color	Color of the slide's canvas, or background
Text and line colors	Contrast colors with the background color; used for text and drawn lines
Shadow color	Color of the shadow of text or other object; generally a darker shade of the background
Title text color	Like the text and line colors, contrast color for slide title with the background color
Fill color	Contrast color with both the background and the text and line colors
Accent colors	Colors used for other objects on slides

QUICK TIP

Click a color button on any Color palette, such as the Text Color button, then click Other Color to add a new color to the button menu.

Annotating slides during a slide show

In PowerPoint, you can show your presentation on any computer screen using Slide Show view. Slide Show view turns your computer into a projector that displays your presentation slide by slide. In Unit 1, you used the Slide Show View button to view the AutoContent slide show. ▶ Lynn runs the president's slide show and practices drawing on a slide so she can teach the president how to annotate slides during the presentation.

1. **Make sure you are viewing Slide 1, then click the Slide Show button**
   The slide show fills the screen with the first slide of the presentation. Lynn advances to the next slide.
2. **Click the mouse button then move the mouse**
   Slide 2 appears on the screen. Moving the mouse displays the pointer and the Annotation icon in the lower-right corner of the screen. You can emphasize major points in your presentation by drawing on the slide during a slide show by using the Annotation tool.
3. **Click the Annotation icon**
   The pointer changes to the Annotation tool, and the Annotation icon changes to the Exit Annotation icon. While the Annotation tool is turned on, mouse clicks do not advance to the next slide.
4. **Position under the title, then drag to draw a line**
   Compare your screen to Figure 4-19. You can draw anything on the slide when the Annotation tool is turned on. To erase the drawing, simply press [E], the letter "E" key. For other slide show controls, see Table 4-3.
5. **Press [E] to erase the annotation drawing**
   The drawing on Slide 2 is erased. Lynn now finishes using the Annotation tool.
6. **Click**
   The Exit Annotation icon changes back to. Lynn uses the mouse to advance through the rest of the presentation.
7. **Click the mouse to move through all the slides in the presentation**
   After clicking the last slide in the presentation, you return to Slide view.

TABLE 4-3: Slide show controls

CONTROL	DESCRIPTION
[E]	Erases the annotation drawing
[W]	Changes the screen to white
[B]	Changes the screen to black
[→]	Advances to the next slide
[←]	Returns to the previous slide
[Esc]	Stops the slide show

FIGURE 4-19: Presentation slide in Slide Show view

Pointer changes to Annotation tool

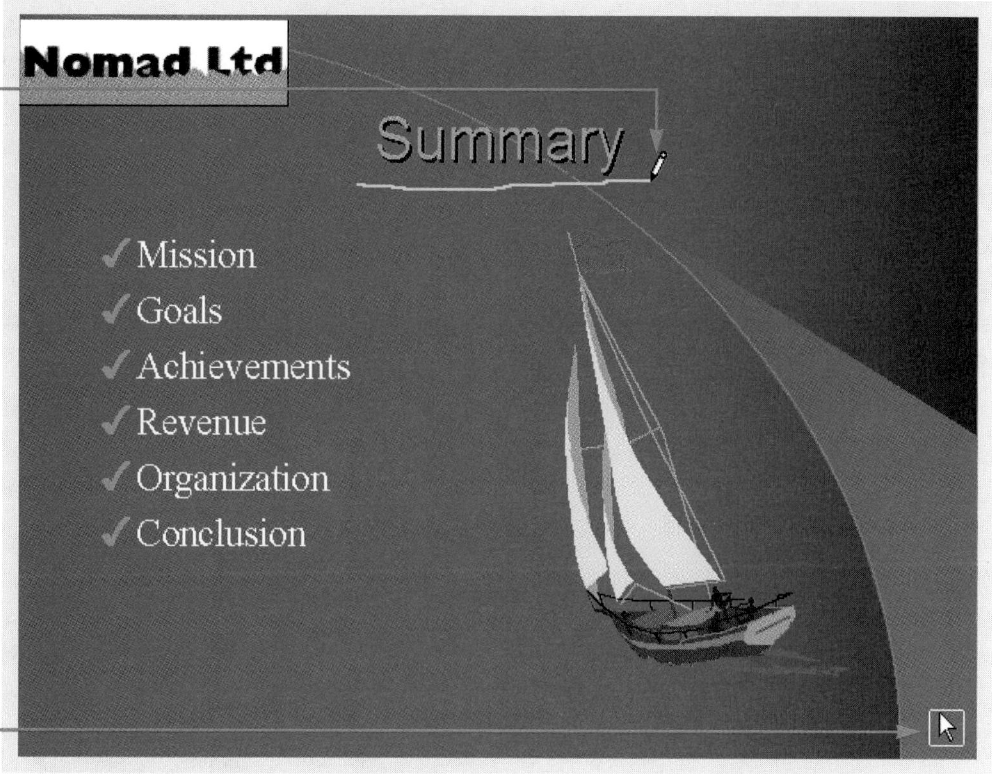

Annotation icon changes to Exit Annotation icon

Showing slide shows on computers without PowerPoint

PowerPoint comes with a special application called **PowerPoint Viewer**. This application allows you to show a slide show on a computer that does not have PowerPoint installed. You can freely install the PowerPoint Viewer program on any compatible system. To install the program, insert the PowerPoint Viewer setup disk into a disk drive, click File on the Program Manager menu bar, click Run, type a:\vsetup (or b:\vsetup) in the File Name text box, then click OK. To run a slide show, double-click the PowerPoint Viewer icon in the Microsoft Office program group to open the Microsoft PowerPoint Viewer dialog box, click a presentation file from the list of filenames, then click Show. You can run a slide show using presentation files from PowerPoint 4.0 for Windows or PowerPoint 4.0 for the Macintosh with the PowerPoint Viewer.

QUICK TIP

Click the Slide Show button to give a slide show beginning with the current slide.

Using slide show special effects

You can add a dramatic element to your slide show presentation by adding special effects to an individual slide or a group of slides. Slide show special effects include transitions, timings, and builds. A **slide transition** is a visual effect applied to a slide show as it moves from one slide to another. **Slide timing** refers to the time a slide appears on the screen. With a **build slide**, you control when bulleted text appears on the screen. ▶ Using the Slide Sorter view, Lynn wants to add slide show special effects to give impact to the president's presentation.

1 Click the **Slide Sorter View button**
The Slide Sorter view displays the slides as miniatures, and the slide you were viewing in Slide view is selected, as shown in Figure 4-20. The number of slides that appear on your screen might be different depending on the current view scale. To add a transition to all the slides, Lynn uses the Select All command to select all the slides quickly.

2 Click **Edit** on the menu bar, then click **Select All**

3 Click the **Transition Effects list arrow** on the Slide Sorter toolbar, then click **Checkerboard Across**
Now, when you move from slide to slide, the Checkerboard Across transition effect will make the transition more interesting. Notice that a transition symbol appears below each slide miniature. Now Lynn applies a build to the two slides that have bulleted lists.

4 Click between the slides to deselect them, click **Slide 4**, press **[Shift]** and click **Slide 5**, click the **Build Effects list arrow** on the Slide Sorter toolbar, then click **Fly From Bottom**
A build symbol appears for Slides 4 and 5. Now she rehearses the timings of the show.

5 Click **Slide 1**, then click the **Rehearse Timings button** on the Slide Sorter toolbar
A small timing box appears in the lower-left corner of the screen with a current accumulated time for the slide. You can click the timing box or the slide to accept the time and continue to the next slide.

6 Click **each slide** to give it a slide time
As you proceed through the show, the time you spent on each slide appears in the timing box. When you reach the build slides, the bullets appear one at a time as you click the slide. At the end of the rehearsal, PowerPoint asks if you want to record the new timings.

7 Click **Yes** to record the new slide timings
Notice that each slide has a timing below it, as shown in Figure 4-21. You can change any slide time later using the Transition command on the Tools menu. Lynn previews the final presentation.

8 Click **View** on the menu bar, click **Slide Show**, click the **Use Slide Timings radio button** in the Advance section, then click **Show**
Looks great! Lynn gives the presentation to Bill Davidson for his review

9 Save and close the presentation, then exit PowerPoint

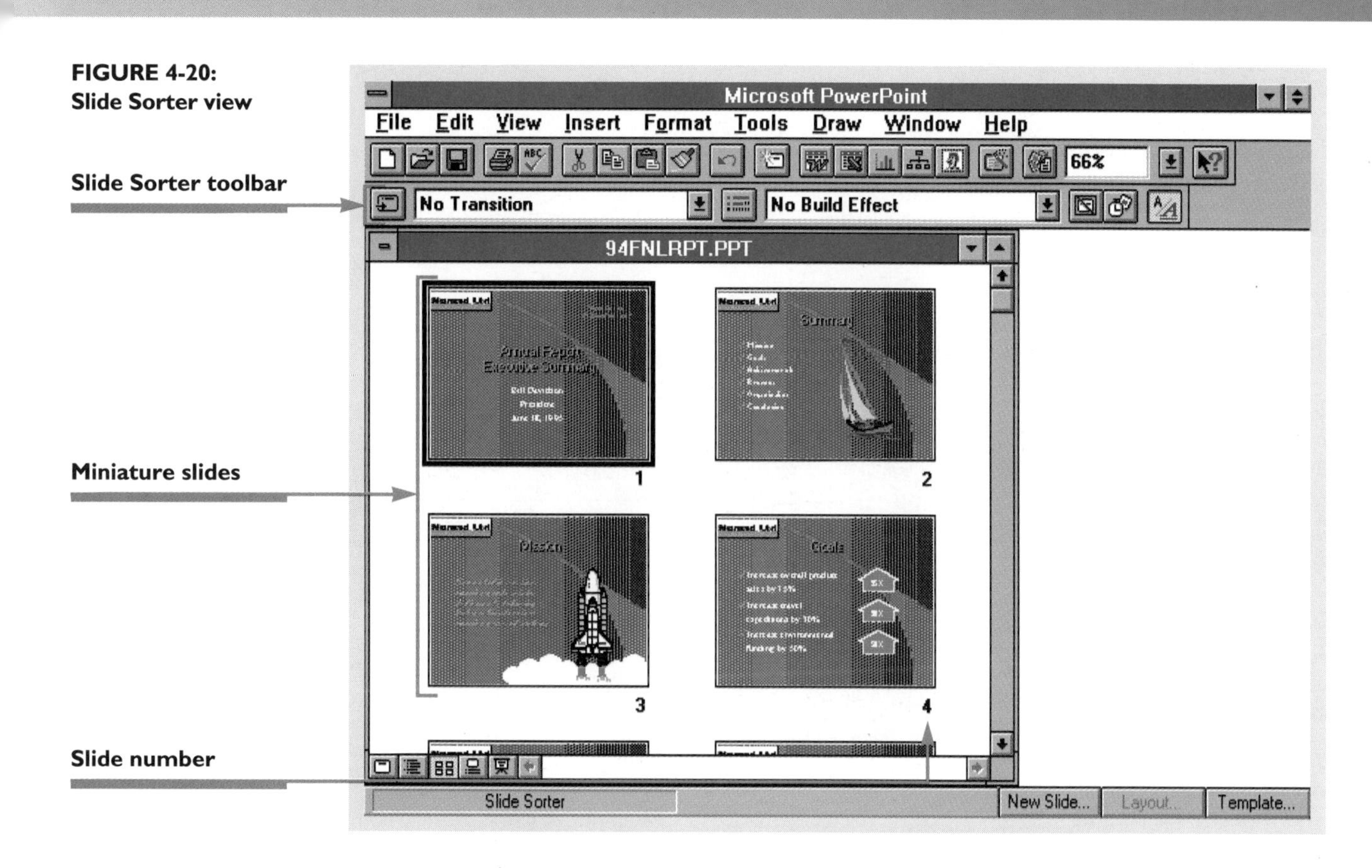

FIGURE 4-20: Slide Sorter view

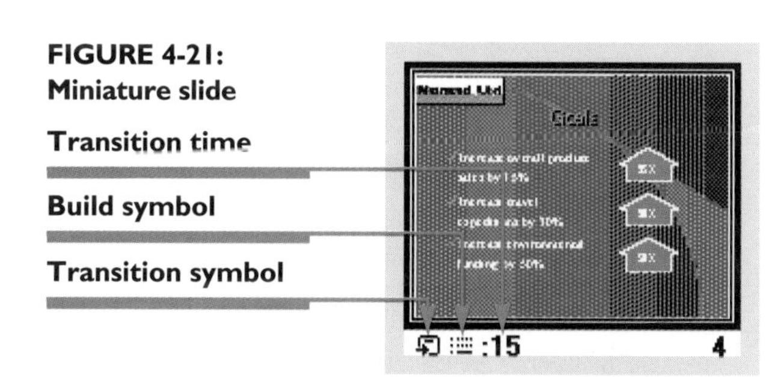

FIGURE 4-21: Miniature slide

Customizing a slide show

You might want to customize a slide show for a specific audience. With PowerPoint, you can hide the slides you don't want to use during a slide show by using the Hide Slide command. In Slide Sorter view, select the slide or slides you want to hide, then click the Hide Slide button on the Slide Sorter toolbar. A small hide symbol appears over the slide number. During a slide show, a Hide icon appears in the lower-right corner of the screen. If you want to see the hidden slide, click the Hide icon; otherwise continue normally.

QUICK TIP

In Slide Sorter view, click the Transition symbol under the miniature slide to see the transition for the slide. See Figure 4-21.

CONCEPTSREVIEW

Label each of the elements of the PowerPoint window shown in Figure 4-22.

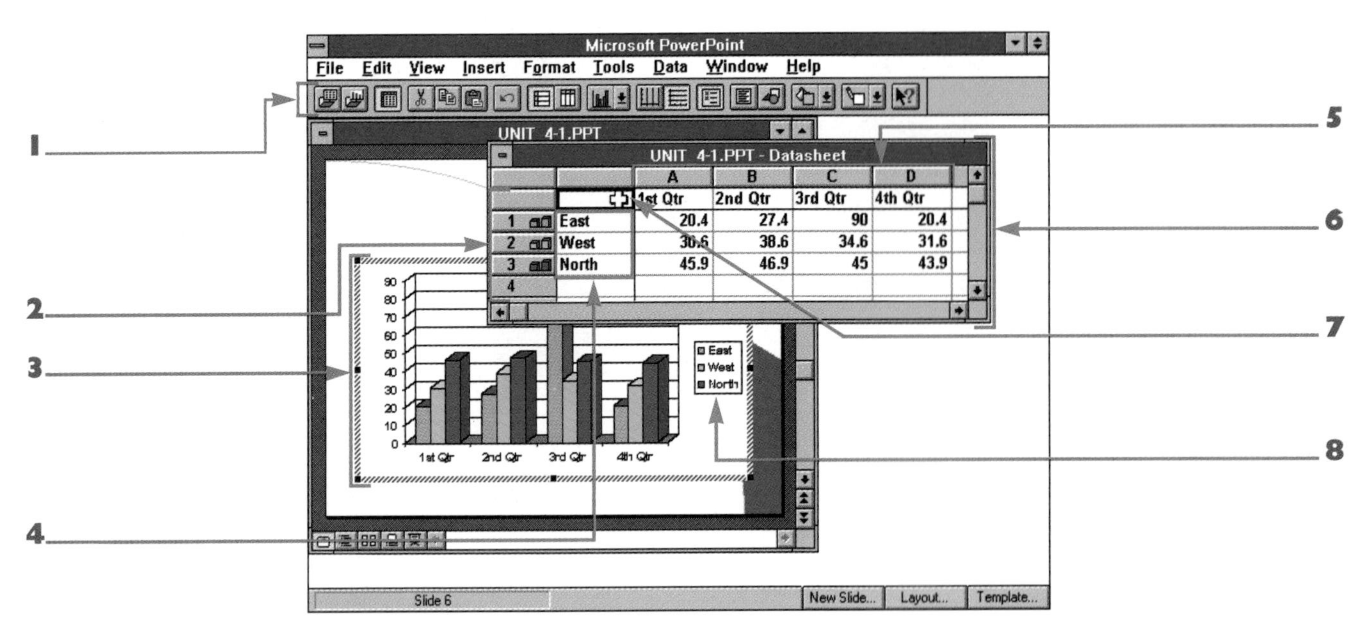

FIGURE 4-22

Match each of the terms with the statement that describes its function.

9 A selected cell in a datasheet

10 A graphical representation of a datasheet

11 The way information appears

12 Contains the data displayed in a chart

13 Maintains a link to another application

a. Chart
b. Embedded object
c. Datasheet
d. Format
e. Active cell

Select the best answer from the list of choices.

14 The PowerPoint clip art is stored in a
a. Folder
b. Gallery
c. Card Catalogue
d. Floppy disk

15 Which is NOT a way to access PowerPoint clip art?
a. Double-click a clip art placeholder
b. Click the Insert Clip Art button
c. Click Clip Art from the Insert menu
d. Double-click the Clip Art icon

16 Which of the following is NOT true about a PowerPoint graph?
a. A graph is made up of a datasheet and chart.
b. You can select a whole row or column by clicking a control box.
c. An active cell has a black selection rectangle around it.
d. You can click a control box to edit the contents of an individual cell.

17 An organizational chart is
a. A PowerPoint slide
b. An embedded object
c. A WordArt box
d. An object

APPLICATIONS REVIEW

1 Insert clip art.

a. Start PowerPoint and open the presentation UNIT_4-2.PPT from your Student Disk, save it as 94SALES.PPT in the MY_FILES directory, then click OK to close the Summary Info dialog box.

b. Click the Next Slide button.

c. Double-click the clip art placeholder.

d. In the Choose a category to view below section, scroll down the list, then click Maps - U.S. If the Maps - U.S. category doesn't appear, select a different category.

e. Click the 3-D U.S. Map with State Boundaries clip art, then click OK.

2 Insert a graph.

a. Click the Next Slide button.

b. Click the Layout button. The Slide Layout dialog box opens.

c. Click the Graph AutoLayout, then click Apply.

d. Double-click the graph placeholder to start Graph.

e. Click the first cell in the datasheet.

f. Click the Import Data button on the Graph Standard toolbar. The Import Data dialog box opens.

g. In the File Name list box, click the worksheet UNIT_4-3.XLS from your Student Disk, then click OK. A Microsoft Graph dialog box opens.

h. Click OK to overwrite the existing data. The data from the Microsoft Excel worksheet overwrites the default data in the Graph datasheet.

i. Click a blank area of the Presentation window to exit Graph.

3 Format a graph.

a. Double-click the graph object.

b. Click the By Column button on the Graph Standard toolbar.

c. Click the datasheet title names on the x-axis, click the Font Size list arrow on the Formatting toolbar, then click 14.

d. Click Insert on the menu bar, click Titles, click the Chart Title check box, then click OK.

e. Type "1994 Regional Sales Figures," then click a blank area below the title.

f. Click a blank area of the Presentation window to exit Graph.

4 Edit an organizational chart.

a. Click the Next Slide button and double-click the organizational chart, then click the maximize button.

b. Click the Subordinate button on the Org Chart toolbar.

c. Click the Production Dept. Manager chart box.

d. In the blank chart box, type "Jordan Shays," press [Tab], then type "Group Lead."

e. Click Edit on the menu bar, click Select, then click All.

f. Click Boxes on the menu bar, click Box Shadow, then click the second shadow option down in the second column.

g. Click File on the menu bar, click Exit and Return to 94SALES.PPT, then click Yes to update the presentation.

5 Work with WordArt to enhance slide text.

a. Click the Next Slide button and click the Layout button, click the Object AutoLayout, then click Apply.

b. Double-click the object placeholder.

c. In the Insert Object dialog box, click the down scroll arrow, click Microsoft WordArt 2.0, then click OK.

d. Type "The OutBack Series," press [Enter], type "by," press [Enter], type "Nomad Ltd," then click Update Display.

e. Click the Format Text list arrow, then click the Slant Up symbol on the bottom row.

f. Click the Shading button on the Formatting toolbar, click the Foreground list arrow, click Red, then click OK.

g. Click the Shadow button on the Formatting toolbar, click the top middle symbol.

h. Click a blank area of the Presentation window to exit WordArt.

6 Change a Slide Master.

a. Click the Next Slide button and click View on the menu bar, click Master, then click Slide Master.

b. Click the first line of text in the master text placeholder.

c. Click Format on the menu bar, click Bullet, then click the "X" in the top row, fourth from the right.

d. Click the Size % of Text up arrow until the percentage reaches 100, then click OK.

e. Click the Slide View button.

7 Change a color scheme.

a. Click Format on the menu bar, then click Slide Color Scheme.

b. Click the Blue Accent color in the Change Scheme Colors section.

c. Click Change Color. The Accent Color dialog box opens.

d. Click the fourth blue color down in the ninth column. Click OK then click Apply to All.

e. Click Format on the menu bar, then click Slide Background.

f. In the Shaded Styles section, click the Vertical radio button.

g. Click the Light scroll arrow three times, then click Apply to All.

8 Add slide show effects.

a. Click the Slide Sorter View button.

b. Click Edit on the menu bar, then click Select All.

c. Click the Transition Effect list arrow on the Slide Sorter toolbar, then click Random Transition.

d. Click the Rehearse Timings button on the Slide Sorter toolbar.

e. Click each slide to give it a time, then click Yes to record the new times.

f. Click between slides to deselect all the slides.

g. Click Slide 2, press [Shift], click the scroll down arrow a few times, then click Slide 6.

h. Click the Build list arrow on the Slide Sorter toolbar, then click Dissolve.

i. Double-click Slide 1.

j. Click View on the menu bar, then click Slide Show.

k. Click the Use Slide Timings radio button in the Advance section, then click Show.

l. Save, print, and then close the presentation.

INDEPENDENT CHALLENGE 1

You are the communications director at Pyles & Todd Design, Inc., an international advertising agency. One of your responsibilities is to create an on-screen presentation to promote the company at the National Association of Advertising Agencies (NAAA) convention. Use Green Pasture Farms quality products and the company's long history as the basis for your presentation.

Plan and create a slide show presentation for the marketing staff to use at the NAAA convention.

Create your own company information, but assume the following: the marketing staff will be using a color monitor with 256 colors.

To complete this independent challenge:

1. Think about the results you want to see, the information you need to create the slide show presentation, and the message you want to communicate.
2. Plan and create the color slide show presentation using slide transitions, build slides, slide timings, and shaded backgrounds. Use the Slide Show command from the View menu to make the slide show presentation run continuously.
3. Save the presentation as NAAA.PPT in the MY_FILES directory on your Student Disk. Make sure you preview the slide show presentation on the computer the marketing staff will use at the convention using PowerPoint or the PowerPoint Viewer.
4. Submit your presentation plan and the final slide show presentation.

INDEPENDENT CHALLENGE 2

You are the teacher at an elementary school. To help your 4th grade class understand the major holidays celebrated throughout the year, you want to create color slides with fun information and art for the students.

Plan and create a color slide presentation for the classroom. Create slides for the major holidays of the school year. Create your own holiday material.

To complete this independent challenge:

1. Think about the results you want to see, the information you need to create the slide show presentation, and the message you want to communicate.
2. Plan and create the color slide presentation using Microsoft ClipArt Gallery and Microsoft WordArt. Use the AutoLayout to help you create slides with the title text, bulleted text, and art. Remember you are creating and entering your own presentation material.
3. Save the presentation as HOLIDAYS.PPT in the MY_FILES directory on your Student Disk. Before printing, preview the file so you know what the presentation will look like. Adjust any items, and then print the slides.
4. Submit your presentation plan and the final slide show presentation.

Glossary

Active cell A selected cell in a Graph datasheet.

Adjustment handle A small diamond positioned next to a resize handle that changes the dimension of an object.

Annotation A freehand drawing on the screen using the Annotation tool. You can annotate only in Slide Show view.

Application A software program, such as Microsoft PowerPoint.

AutoContent wizard Helps you get your presentation started by creating a sample outline using information you provide.

AutoLayout A predesigned slide layout that contains placeholder layouts for titles, main text, clip art, graphs, and charts.

Blinking insertion point Vertical blinking line in a text object that shows your current location and where text can be entered.

Build slide Known as a progressive disclosure slide, a build slide reveals bullet points separately during a slide show.

Bullet A small graphic symbol, often used to identify a line of text in a list.

Cell A rectangle in a Graph datasheet where you enter data.

Chart The component of a graph that graphically portrays your Graph datasheet information.

Clip Art Professionally designed pictures that come with PowerPoint.

Color scheme The basic eight colors that make up a PowerPoint presentation. For example, a color scheme has a separate color for text, lines, and background color. You can change the color scheme on any presentation at any time.

Control boxes The gray boxes located along the left and top of a Graph datasheet.

Cue Cards A step-by-step instruction guide that gives you information on how to accomplish a specific task. Cue Cards appear in a separate window and stay on your screen while you work through the task instructions.

Datasheet The component of a graph that contains the information you want to display on your Graph chart.

Dialog box A box that displays the available command options for you to review or change.

Directory A subdivision of a disk that works like a filing system to help you organize files.

Disable To turn an option or feature off.

Drive The mechanism in a computer that turns a disk to retrieve and store information. Personal computers often have one hard drive labeled C and two drives labeled A and B that read removable floppy disks.

Dotted selection box Indicates that an object is selected and can be modified.

Elevator The scroll box in the vertical scroll bar.

Embedded object An object that is created in another application but is stored in PowerPoint. Embedded objects maintain a link to their original application for easy editing.

Formatting toolbar The toolbar that contains buttons for the most frequently used formatting commands, such as font type and size.

Gallery A visual index that stores the PowerPoint clip art into categories.

Global change A change made to an entire selection.

Graph The datasheet and chart you create to graphically display information.

Grid Evenly spaced horizontal and vertical lines that do not appear on the slide.

Main text Sub points or bullet points under a title in Outline view.

Main text placeholder A reserved box on a slide for the main text points.

Master text placeholder The placeholder on the Slide Master that controls the formatting and placement of the Main text placeholder on each slide. If you modify the Master text placeholder, each Main text placeholder is affected in the entire presentation.

Master title placeholder The placeholder on the Slide Master that controls the formatting and placement of the Title placeholder on each slide. If you modify the Master title placeholder, each Title placeholder is affected in the entire presentation.

Menu bar The horizontal bar below the title bar that contains the PowerPoint commands. Click a menu name to display a list of commands.

Object The component you place or draw on a slide. Objects are drawn lines and shapes, text, clip art, imported pictures, and embedded objects.

Organizational chart A diagram of connected boxes that shows reporting structure.

Outlining toolbar The toolbar that contains buttons for the most used outlining commands, such as moving and indenting text lines.

Pick a Look Wizard Helps you choose a professional look for your presentation. You can use the Pick a Look wizard at any time.

Placeholder A dashed line box where you place text or objects.

PowerPoint Viewer A special application designed to run a PowerPoint slide show on any compatible computer that does not have PowerPoint installed.

PowerPoint window A window that contains the running PowerPoint application. The PowerPoint window displays the PowerPoint menus, toolbars, and Presentation window.

Presentation graphics application A software program used to organize and present information.

Presentation window The area or "canvas" where you work and view your presentation. You type text and work with objects in the Presentation window.

Resize handle The small square at each corner of a selected object. Dragging a resize handle resizes the object.

Scale To resize a picture or object by a specified percentage.

Scroll To move within a window to see more of the window contents.

Slanted line selection box A box that appears around a text object indicating it is selected and ready to enter or edit text.

Slide icon A symbol used to identify a slide title in Outline view.

Slide Indicator box A small box that appears when you drag the elevator in Slide and Note Pages view. This box identifies which slide you are on.

Stacking order The order in which objects are placed on the slide. The first object placed on the slide is on the bottom while the last object placed on the slide is on the top.

Standard toolbar The row of buttons, or toolbar, that perform the most frequently used commands, such as copy and paste.

Status bar Located at the bottom of the PowerPoint window, it displays messages about what you are doing and seeing in PowerPoint, such as the current slide number or a description of a command or button.

Text box A box within a dialog box where you type information needed to carry out a command.

Text object Any text you create with the Text Tool or enter into a placeholder. Once you enter text into a placeholder, the placeholder becomes a text object.

Text label A text object you create with the Text Tool that does not automatically wrap text inside a box.

Timing The time a slide stays on the screen during a slide show.

Title The first line or heading in Outline view.

Title bar The horizontal bar at the top of the window that displays the name of the document or the application.

Title placeholder A reserved box on a slide for a presentation or slide title.

Title slide The first slide in your presentation.

Toggle button A button that turns a feature on and off.

Toolbar A graphical bar with buttons that perform certain PowerPoint commands, such as opening and saving.

ToolTip When you place the pointer over a button, a small box appears that identifies the button by name.

Transition The effect that moves one slide off the screen and the next slide on the screen during a slide show. Each slide can have its own transition effect.

TrueType font A font that can be displayed or printed at any size.

View PowerPoint has five views that allow you to look at your presentation in different ways. Each view allows you to change and modify the content of your presentation differently.

View buttons Appear at the bottom of the Presentation window. Allow you to switch between PowerPoints' five views.

Window A rectangle area on your screen where you view and work on presentations.

Wizard A guided approach that steps you through creating a presentation. PowerPoint has two wizards, the AutoContent Wizard and the Pick a Look Wizard, that help you with the content and the look of your presentation.

Word processing box A text object you draw with the Text Tool that automatically wraps text inside a box.

Index

SPECIAL CHARACTERS

A

B

C

D

E

F

G

N

O

P

W

Z